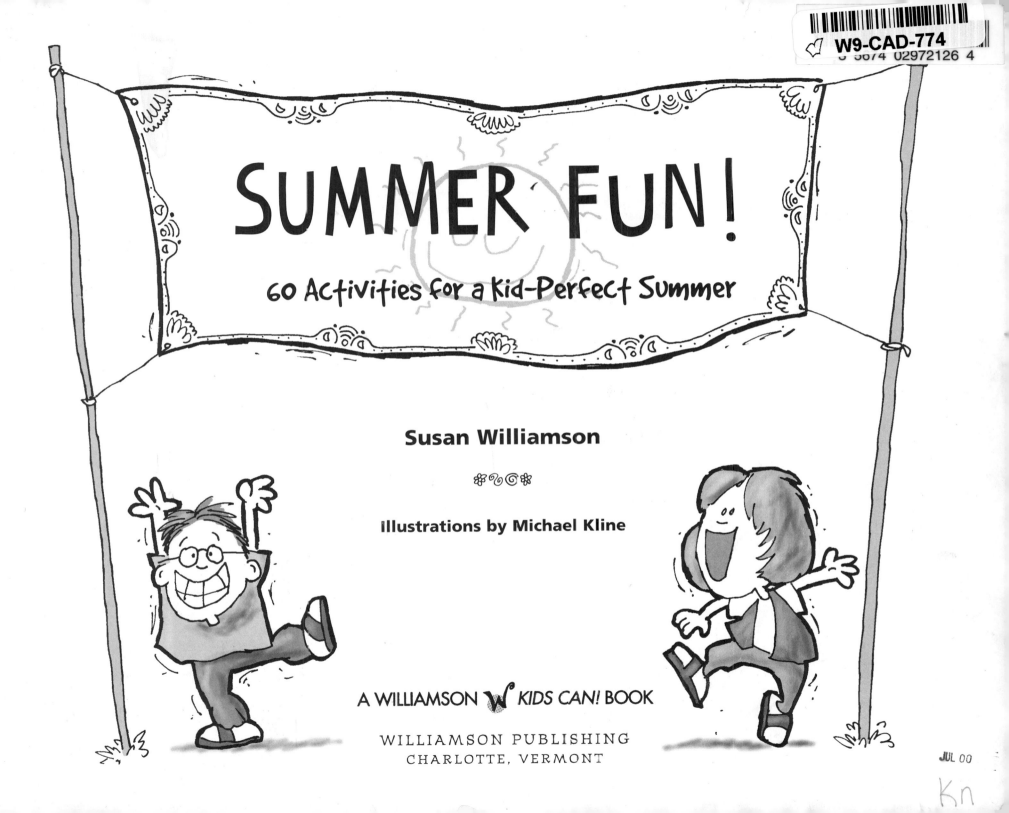

SUMMER FUN!

60 Activities for a Kid-Perfect Summer

Susan Williamson

✿❧◎✿

Illustrations by Michael Kline

A WILLIAMSON **W** KIDS CAN! BOOK

WILLIAMSON PUBLISHING
CHARLOTTE, VERMONT

Kids Can!®, *Little Hands*®, and *Tales Alive*® are registered trademarks of
Williamson Publishing Company. *Kaleidoscope Kids*™ and *Good Times*™ are
trademarks of Williamson Publishing Company.

LIBRARY OF CONGRESS CATALOGING-IN-PUBLICATION DATA

Williamson, Susan Soloway
    Summer Fun! : 60 activities for a kid-perfect summer / Susan S. Williamson
        p. cm.
        "A Williamson kids can! book"
    Includes index.
    Summary: Suggests a variety of activities for summertime, including nature
study, cooking, crafts, games, creative activities, and more.
    ISBN 1-885593-33-3 (alk. paper)
    1. Amusements — Juvenile literature. 2. Creative activities and seat work —
Juvenile literature. [1. Amusements. 2. Games. 3. Handicraft.]
    I. Title: Summer fun!
      GV1203.W673 1999
      790.1'922—dc21   98-53269
                            CIP
                            AC

KIDS CAN!® CONCEPT AND SERIES EDITOR: Susan Williamson

INTERIOR DESIGN: Bonnie Atwater, Atwater Design

ILLUSTRATIONS: Michael P. Kline, Michael P. Kline Illustrations

COVER DESIGN: Trezzo-Braren Studio

PRINTING: Capital City Press

Williamson Publishing Co.
P.O. Box 185
Charlotte, Vermont 05445
1-800-234-8791

Manufactured in the United States of America

10 9 8 7 6 5 4 3 2

Permission to use the following recipes and/or activities is granted by
Williamson Publishing Company: from *Ancient Greece!* by Avery Hart & Paul
Mantell: page 8; *Adventures in Art* by Susan Milord: pages 38, 73, 100;
Boredom Busters! by Avery Hart & Paul Mantell: pages 24-26, 39, 40, 56, 58, 80,
83, 101,122, 124, 128; *Fun with My 5 Senses* by Sarah Williamson: page 69;
Gifts for the Baby by Cindy Higgins: page 97; *Hands Around the World* by
Susan Milord: pages 3, 11; *Making Cool Crafts & Awesome Art* by Roberta Gould:
pages 44, 99; *Kids' Computer Creations* by Carol Sabbeth: pages 10, 48;
Kids' Crazy Art Concoctions by Jill Hauser: pages 12, 14, 19; *Kids Create!* by
Laurie Carlson: page 92; *Kids Cook!* by Sarah and Zachary Williamson: pages 21,
42; *Kids Make Music!* by Avery Hart & Paul Mantell: page 108; *The Kids'
Multicultural Art Book* by Alexandra Terzian: page 126; *The Kids' Multicultural
Cookbook* by Deanna Cook: pages 63, 120; *The Kids' Nature Book* by Susan
Milord: page 54; *The Kids' Wildlife Book* by Warner Shedd: page 37; *Tales of the
Shimmering Sky* by Susan Milord: pages 50, 51, 76-78, 81, 112.

To paraphrase: A book a day helps keep illiteracy away.

Reading books aloud and reading instructions or how-to-do-it books (such as this one) aloud are all part of the solution.

As soon as you learn to read, join in the effort. Share your reading power with someone every day!

ACKNOWLEDGEMENTS

I have had the privilege of working with wonderful authors and educators, among many others, over the past 18 years. I would particularly like to thank authors Avery Hart, Paul Mantell, and Susan Milord for their contributions to this book, for their enthusiasm and warmth toward children, and for joining me in this effort on behalf of kids and literacy.

The authors and editors I have worked with at Williamson have taught me a lot about the art of collaboration and have generously allowed me to share on these pages some activities that we have all developed together along the way. Thank you to Williamson authors Laurie Carlson, Deanna Cook, Nancy Fyke, Roberta Gould, Jill Hauser, Sandi Henry, Cindy Higgins, Lynn Nejam, Vicki Overstreet, Judy Press, Carol Sabbeth, Warner Shedd, Golde Soloway, Alexandra Terzian, Sarah Williamson, and Zachary Williamson, and to Williamson editors Vicky Congdon, Jennifer Ingersoll, and Emily Stetson.

Thank you to Michael Kline, who brings such insight and poignancy to the Kline kids that he draws. His illustrations have brightened many a day in our offices. Having never met Michael personally, I am beginning to think that he not only sees the world through the eyes of a 10-year-old, but that he actually *is* a 10-year-old in disguise!

Thank you to Bonnie Atwater, book designer, for understanding what summer fun is and joining in the spirit of this book so wholeheartedly.

Thank you to Ken Braren and Loretta Trezzo Braren for once again capturing the spirit of a book in their wonderful cover design. Theirs is a very special talent indeed.

Thank you to Elizabeth Bluemle, of the Flying Pig Children's Bookstore in Charlotte, Vermont, and to Katherine Chase, librarian at Charlotte Central School, for keeping us informed about kid-favorite literature.

And, most especially, thank you to Jack, Sarah, and Zachary—my gentle, but persistent, teachers and partners in life.

Susan Williamson

CONTENTS

SUMMER FUN!

THREE CHEERS! IT'S SUMMERTIME!

YAY!

the plan

Summer's here! Yahoo! School's out! Hip, hip, hooray! Stay up later at night, sleep later in the morning, loll around in the sun, have your friends over, maybe even go to sports camp for a few days. Yes, this is it. The perfect summer! Ah, yeah!

What's that? You've been out of school three days, and what? No way. Did I hear that right? No, it can't be. You're out of school three days and you're bored? BORED? B O R E D ?

Well, you know what? Almost everyone finds that too much free time is almost as bad as no free time. Funny how when you've got homework to do you can think of dozens of things you'd much rather be doing. Then, when you have whole weeks free and clear, nothing sounds very exciting. Well, let's do something about it—now!

Make a Plan—the Fun Will Follow!

A *plan*? Sounds strange, but a little bit of a schedule helps put some order in your day and—almost like magic—everything is so much nicer! The fun will follow, because making a plan puts *you* in charge of your day. And, when you are in charge, we feel certain there will be lots of silly summer days!

We've made it easy for you to fill your days (and banish the "B" word): There are things to do on rainy days (pages 52-74), on absolutely picture-perfect sunny days (almost this whole book!), when you are on your own (pages 90-105), and even when you are having one of those ants-in-your-pants days when nothing's quite right (1-21; 106-120)! Extend your fun days into those special summer nights (pages 75-89) and don't forget to celebrate the outdoors (pages 22-40; 121-132), too.

Make This the GREATEST!

So, get **going**, get **crowing**, get **grinning**, get **giggling**—and let's get this swinging summer **moving** and **grooving**. Yes sirree, this is going to be the **greatest** summer (until the next one) ever! **Happy summer, kiddo!**

Make It Happen!

Will this be your best summer ever? We certainly hope so! After all, you are a hard-working kid—and we really do know that being a kid, going to school, and having lots of day-to-day responsibilities is very hard work! So, let's get in gear, because we're here to help you make it happen. Here's to the very best summer ever!

★ **Do something!** Duh. Sounds so obvious, but doing something, doing most *anything*, like baking cookies, or looking at some photos or playing a board game, turns ho-hum into fun. Grumbling about nothing to do turns into . . . well . . . sitting around mumbling about nothing to do!

★ **Be flexible!** If one plan doesn't work, then take a moment to think of something else to do. If it rains on a beach day, shift gears to indoor fun. Let's see that grin no matter what!

★ **Chores, chores, chores!** Here's the scoop on that: Get them done first thing in the morning and then feel very good about rewarding yourself with some super summer fun all day long!

★ **Playing with the sibs**: If you have little sisters or brothers who always want you to play with them, set a time and tell them what you will do and for how long. (Make a paper plate clock and set the hands for the time you will play with them; that way, they can compare to a real clock without pestering you.) The rest of the time, you can be on your own!

★ **Mix it up!** A little silliness, a little active time, a little quiet time. Time with friends, time alone, time with your dog. Play some knock-knock jokes, read a book, climb a tree, shoot some baskets, or make some art.

★ **Get out & about!** Going somewhere new and different doesn't have to cost anything: Go to the airport, the library, the park, to an outdoor concert, a street fair. If you need a grown-up with you, then plan ahead. Look through this book for lots of "Out & About" ideas.

★ **Have super summer fun!** Double duh. After all, that's what this book is all about!

Promises, Promises!

You can keep a promise, of course. We hope you feel comfortable making and keeping this summertime promise:

I promise that I will take good care of myself this summer. I'll eat yummy foods that are good for me, slather on sunscreen, get lots of physical exercise, enjoy some quiet time, play in safe areas, follow my family's rules, and always tell them where I am and who I am with.

SILLY SUMMER FUN

Break out the sillies! In summer, you can let silliness reign supreme, so act out those amazing antics, let the comedian in you burst forth, make zaniness part of every day, giggle, guffaw, laugh, and be a clown, be a clown, BE A CLOWN! Whatever you do, let those sillies loose!

WEIRD-WALKING AND HIGH-STEPPING KIDS

For pure, simple, giggly fun, try walking on stilts and can-walkers. Be sure to capture the sight on a camera or camcorder, because the only thing more fun than being on stilts is watching yourself on them!

CRAZY CAN-WALKERS

May we suggest that you take a tour of your very own backyard or street on your own two feet—"canned feet," that is!
Clomp, clomp, clomp . . .

MATERIALS

- ◆ 2 cans of the same size (48-ounce/1.5-L juice cans are good)
- ◆ Can openers, both punch-type and rotating
- ◆ 6 to 8 feet (2 to 3 m) of rope, cut in two equal lengths

LET'S DO IT!

1. Remove the top from each can. Punch two holes near the closed end of each can, just below the rim, directly across from each other. Thread the rope through the holes and knot it securely.
2. To use, stand on the end near the holes, and hold the ropes in each hand. Try walking, letting your arms do the lifting. You'll soon get the hang of it!

STAGGERING STILT-WALKERS!

If you think making your stilts is the easy part, well, you are absolutely right! But with a little practice, a lot of laughs, and definitely some tumbles, you'll be a giant in your own backyard. How's the weather up there?

P.S. Be sure to ask a grown-up to help you with the tools.

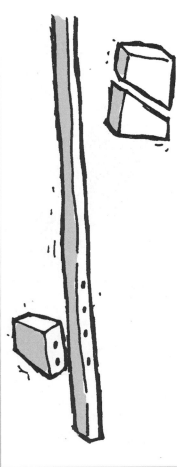

MATERIALS

◆ Handsaw

◆ 6-inch (15-cm) piece of a 2x4

◆ Drill

◆ 2 lengths of lumber (2x3s are perfect), cut only a little longer than you are tall

◆ 4 to 6 wood screws, about 3 inches (7.5 cm)

◆ Sandpaper

LET'S DO IT!

Cut the 2x4 in half as shown above to make footrests. Then, drill two holes in each footrest and a series of corresponding holes along the lower length of each stilt. Starting low, attach the footrests with the screws. Sand the edges and any rough spots.

To use your stilts: Stand on a step, wrap your arms around the stilts, and step on the footrests. Keep your legs snugly against the stilts and think of them as extensions of your legs. Now, try walking slowly. Practice on a grassy area.

YAY!

...out & about

Going to the circus is great, silly summer fun! Call the local Chamber of Commerce or your state's Department of Tourism to find out if there are any circuses coming to town this summer. Save your money to buy a ticket and encourage some friends to do the same. Before you know it, the lights will dim, the circus band will strike up a tune, and clowns, elephants, horses, acrobats, tightrope-walkers, and stilt-walkers will all be in the ring with their glittering costumes and big smiles. Welcome, ladies and gentlemen, and children of all ages . . .

Have a Circus Parade!

Calling all can-clompers and stilt-walkers! Acrobats and jugglers, too! Drum-beaters, kazoo-players and tambourine-shakers, baton-twirlers and ribbon-flutterers! Come one, come all for the neighborhood circus parade. Get out the face paints (see page 12), and pull on some mismatched, oversized clothes and frumpy hats. Put ribbons and party hats on your dogs, wind crepe paper through your bicycles' wheels, and make a banner. Get a drumbeat going (ta-dum, ta-dum, ta-dum-dum-dum), step right out, and let the circus parade begin!

Books can take you just about anywhere, including inside the circus. If you like the circus, you'll certainly enjoy reading *Emmeline at the Circus* by Marjorie Priceman. And if you think you might like circus life, you might find *Amanda Joins the Circus* by Avi interesting.

YO-YOS AND BOOMERANGS

Do you know the saying

"There is nothing new under the sun"?

Well, we happen to think that every time a baby

is born, something unique comes into this world.

Nevertheless, it is always a surprise to learn

how "old" some of our "new" inventions are.

You'll be surprised at how long yo-yos and

boomerangs have been around,

keeping kids happy on gentle summer days.

Invent a Toy or Game

Yeah, right! Hula hoops, yo-yos, checkers, jacks, slides, see-saws — they all seem so simple to us now. Everyone plays with them, even our parents (can you imagine?) played with them. Yet, *someone* invented them — so why not you?

Many inventions are the result of one person or a group of people sitting around, thinking of something to do, and using the materials at hand. Usually, the simpler, the better; the fewer the parts, the less it costs to produce, and the more people can play with it without it breaking.

So, put on your thinking caps and try to come up with a new game, a new challenge, or a simple toy that people will want to play with for years to come.

... out & about

check out world yo-yo records.

Go to the library or bookstore, and look up the world record for longest time spent yo-yoing without stopping in *The Guinness Book of World Records*. Do you think you can beat that record? Look at some of the other records held in sports or whatever interests you. Then, get a group of friends together, and see what records you can set.

MAKE A YO-YO

Although the word *yo-yo* was coined only in 1920 in America, this beloved toy has been around for oh, so very much longer. Kids in ancient Egypt played with yo-yos 5,000 years ago! Kids in ancient Greece probably knew how to "sleep" and "walk the dog," because they played with yo-yos, too!

◆ Roll Model Magic (from an art supply store) into as perfectly round a ball as you can manage, about the size of your palm. Slice two lines around the sphere, as far apart as your pinkie. Gently pull out the slice, leaving room for the string to be wound.

◆ Let dry, and paint using bright colors. Or, how about drawing leaping dolphins that chase each other when the yo-yo spins?

◆ Tie on a 2-foot (60-cm) string (longer won't work), and "yo" away!

Patricia... Are you walking the dog?

Yesssss....

BOOMERANGS

There'll be no losing this wacky toy. Throw the flat, curved shape, invented by the Aboriginal people of Australia more than 10,000 years ago, and watch it come right back to you!

FOLD

Double

To make a boomerang: Trace and cut the boomerang shape from a folded piece of stiff cardboard. Decorate with markers or paint. Try making several sizes and shapes. Toss and compare how they soar. Can you make one come back to you?

summer reads

Get in on the summer action by reading Barbara Dugan's *Loop the Loop* or ask at your library for *Boomerang Hunter* by Jim Kjelgaard.

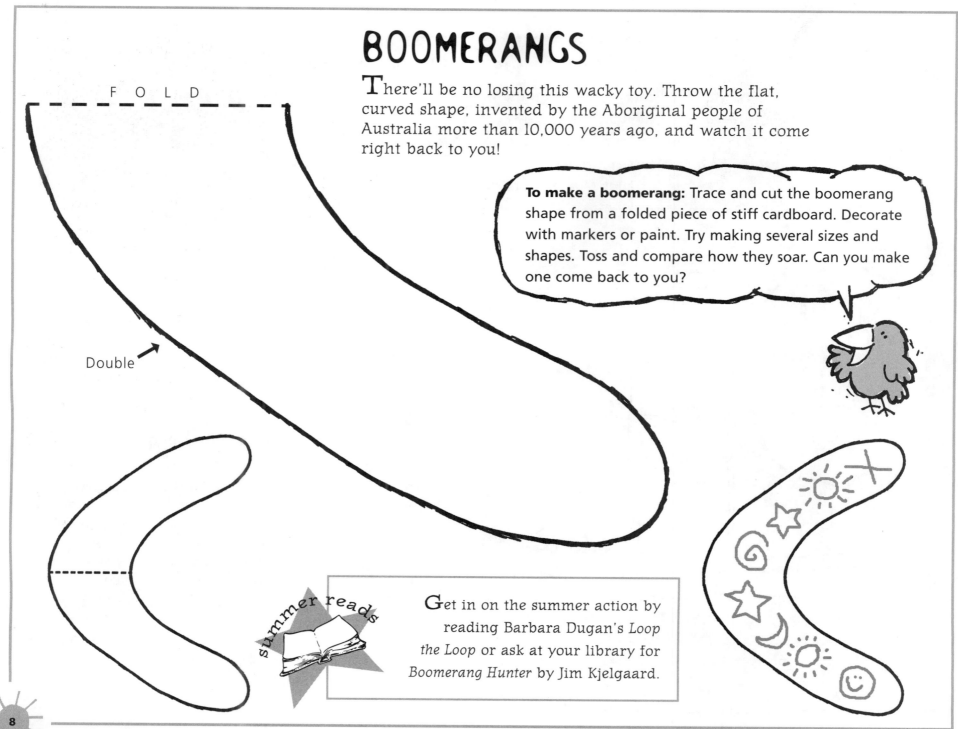

Fresh HOMEMADE LEMONADE!

Why is it that when we dream about hot summer days, we always want to complete the picture with a tall glass of icy-cold homemade lemonade? Well, here it is, picture perfect, at your service.

Tart, cold, and refreshing: In a large glass, combine the juice of 1 lemon (about $1/3$ cup/75 ml), 1 cup (250 ml) of cold water, and 5 teaspoons (25 ml) of sugar. Stir well so the sugar doesn't sit on the bottom of the glass. Pour over ice cubes.

Makes 1 glass

RIDDLE FORTUNE COOKIES

These cookies are fun to make, and just as much fun to watch other people enjoy! Riddles and fortune-telling should be zany and silly, so let loose with your very own brand of humor!

The early bird gets the worm.

★BECAUSE 7, 8, 9!

That's the answer; now you think of the question! And then have fun with some super silly riddles.

INGREDIENTS

¼ cup (50 ml) all-purpose flour
2 tablespoons (25 ml) sugar
1 tablespoon (15 ml) cornstarch
Dash of salt
2 tablespoons (25 ml) cooking oil
1 egg white
1 tablespoon (15 ml) water

LET'S DO IT!

For the cookies:

1. In a small mixing bowl, stir together flour, sugar, cornstarch, and salt. Add oil and egg white; stir until smooth. Add water and mix well.
2. With a grown-up's help, heat a lightly greased skillet. Pour about a tablespoon (15 ml) of batter into the skillet. Spread batter into a 3½-inch (8.5-cm) circle. Cook over low heat 4 minutes or until lightly browned. Flip cookie with wide spatula and cook 1 minute more.
3. Working quickly, place cookie on a pot holder or paper towel. Put a riddle strip in the center (fold paper if necessary). Fold cookie in half; then, fold again over the edge of a glass. Let cool. Repeat with remaining batter.

Makes 8 cookies

★ *Question: Why was 6 afraid of 7?*

LET'S DO IT!

For the riddles:

1. Think of about eight riddles. The sillier, the better! Here are two riddles to get you started:

   What do you call the fear of tight chimneys?
   Answer: Santa Claustrophobia!

   What is a snake's favorite subject in school?
   Answer: Hissssstory!

2. Type the riddle questions, one on a line, on a computer or write them by hand.
3. Cut the questions into strips. Jot the answers down on the back, or leave the answers out. Set aside the strips to place inside the cookies.

For more inspiration, read *Creepy, Crawly Critter Riddles* by Joanne E. Bernstein.

Words of Wisdom in Small Places

People all over the world enjoy reading fortunes and riddles, but half the fun is the package the bits of wisdom come in. Fortune cookies aren't the only places you'll find hidden messages. Next time you go to a restaurant or diner, look at the sugar packets on the table or the tag on the tea bag. These are just two other places you may find a surprise.

THERE IS ABSOLUTELY NOTHING TO DO!

Thinking Up Your Own Riddles

Having trouble thinking up riddles? Here's an idea to help get you started: Think of the riddle as a simple joke and make up the punch line first; then, make up the riddle to fit the punch line. For instance, let's say you think "bratwurst" is a funny word that might make a good answer to a riddle. What could be the riddle? How about, "What do you call a naughty sausage?" — that's right, a bratwurst! Here are a few more:

What kind of cheese is made in Scotland?
Answer: Loch Ness Muenster!

What do you get when you stack hundreds of pizzas on top of one another?
Answer: The leaning tower of pizza!

Where do the people of India go for a sandwich?
Answer: To the New Delhi!

BODY PAINTING

Face painting is always great fun, but the summer sillies shout out "body painting time!" That's right—from the tip of your nose to the tips of your toes, paint away. These paints are easy to make, and they wash right off, so don't be shy. Let loose, get messy, and then hose down. Grab a friend and double the fun. Switch your imagination into high gear and go for it!

MATERIALS

★ Muffin tin or small paper cups
★ 6 teaspoons (30 ml) cornstarch
★ 3 teaspoons (15 ml) cold cream
★ Food coloring
★ Small paintbrushes

LET'S DO IT!

For each color, in its own cup, mix 1 teaspoon (5 ml) cornstarch, ½ teaspoon (2 ml) cold cream, ½ teaspoon (2 ml) water, and a few drops of food coloring. Stir well. Then, dip your brush in and start designing!

Artist's Choice!

There's no end to ideas and styles for body painting. Do you like small and sweet? Try a rainbow brightening your cheek. Are you a stegosaurus wanna-be? Now's your chance! How about a bold tattoo on your back or a diamondback snake curling up your leg? Go for whatever suits your fancy!

Tattoos ⇨

Paint a small picture on your friends' cheeks or on your own arm. Try animals, thunderbolts, sun, moon, a rainbow, or flowers.

⇧ Masks

Instead of drawing a small zebra tattoo on your cheek, become the zebra with paint stripes across your face! Give yourself an animal nose, eyes, and mouth. Try making animals, superheroes, monsters, or clowns.

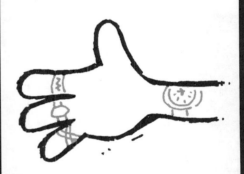

⇦ Wearables

Paint a necklace around your neck, a wristwatch on your arm, or sandals on your feet.

Hand puppets ⇨

Make a fist. See how your tucked-in thumb looks like the lower jaw of a face? Paint your hand to look like a creature. Make finger puppets by giving each finger a special painted personality.

Hi!

Clown faces ⇨

Did you know that every clown has his or her own special face design, called a "working face"? Design your own — happy, sad, angry, or scared, depending on how you feel and what you want to communicate.

Scary Stuff!

Conjure up a frightful face with these crazy concoctions.

Blood = Corn syrup + red food coloring

Warts = Corn syrup + puffed cereal

Beard = Corn syrup + coffee grounds

White hair = Flour. Dust your hair with a handful.

Creepy skin = Unflavored gelatin + water. Use plain or add food coloring. Rub globs on your face.

Thank you, Jill Hauser, for all your wonderful body painting and Gooblek concoctions (page 19).

make a difference

Raise cash for causes!

Whether it's raising money to plant some new trees in the park or to donate to the local food shelf, face painting is a great way to make a difference. Decide on several designs (thunderbolts, rainbows, flowers), put up a sign saying how much for each design and what the money is going to be used for, and then have some fun! (Be sure you know something about the "cause," because people will ask you for the scoop.) Ask if you can set up a face-painting booth outside a grocery store, in the park, at a fair, or in front of the library or town hall.

FACE PAINTING $1 TO HELP THE LIBRARY

BUBBLIN' OVER

Get your silly streak in gear with these wacky and wonderful bubbles. Wave some weird wands and blow some beautiful bubbles—the bigger, the better.

BUBBLE BREW

With this bubble brew, you'll be amazed at the bubbles you can make— and catch! Extra-good news: In the humid weather of summer, bubbles last longer!

INGREDIENTS

4 cups (1 L) water

2 cups (500 ml) liquid dish detergent

2 cups (500 ml) glycerin (available in most drugstores)

2 teaspoons (10 ml) sugar or corn syrup

LET'S DO IT!

Mix the water, detergent, glycerin, and corn syrup in a large basin or dishpan. Make wands and bubble blowers as pictured, using hangers, cans, wire, straws, and string.

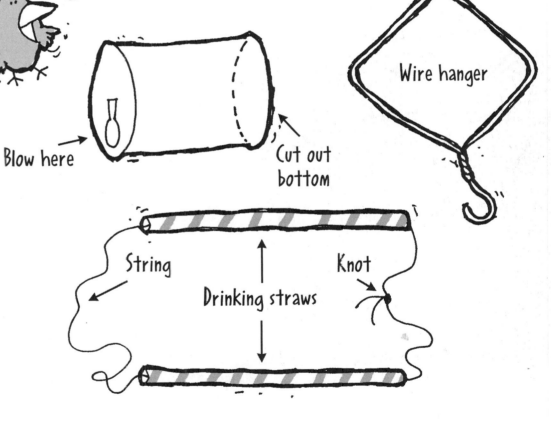

Blow here

Cut out bottom

Wire hanger

String

Drinking straws

Knot

GIANT BUBBLE WANDS

Want to create really huge bubbles? Use two drinking straws and a length of string about 48 inches (1.2 m) long. Thread the string through both straws and knot the ends. Lay the straws and string down in the soap solution. Gently lift up the straws, one in each hand. Spread the straws apart as you lift, and watch a giant bubble form. Wave your arms gently in the air, setting the bubble free to float up, up, and away!

make a difference

Share the bubbles!

Do you know someone who could use a little silliness in his or her life? Bubble fun is great for shaking the sillies out of people of all ages—toddler to oldster. So, whip up some bubble brew, make a few wands, and encourage some people to bubble away. Can't get them to join in? Just start bubbling yourself. The others will be bubbling right by your side before you know it!

Capture a Bubble

Have you ever wished you could save a bubble? Well, you may not be able to prevent a bubble from popping, but you *can* save its print.

MATERIALS

- Tempera paint
- Water
- Liquid dish detergent
- Paper
- Plastic container
- Newspaper
- Drinking straw

LET'S DO IT!

1. Outdoors, make a mixture of bubble brew consistency with a little tempera, some water, and the dish detergent. Stir. (For a brighter color, add more tempera.)

2. Set the container on the ground. Gently blow the straw in the paint mixture. (DO NOT SUCK IN. The mixture tastes horrible and will make you sick!) Keep blowing until the bubbles overflow.

3. To capture a bubble print, gently lay a piece of paper on top of the bubbles. They'll leave a print on your paper before they burst.

4. Repeat with different colors if you wish. Then, lay the paper flat to dry.

What Is a Bubble?

Bubbles are extremely thin layers of soapy water wrapped around puffs of air. Soap helps water stretch out, so once you have a stretchy film, you can fill it with air by blowing on it—just like bubble gum! What makes bubbles pop? Holes! Holes happen when something dry, like your hand, touches the fragile film. Even dust can pop a bubble!

POP!

SILLY SUMM

Some summer days, it's just too hot to do most anything except play around with water. Here are some great ways to cool down.

SLIP 'N' SLIDE

Running through the sprinkler always feels great, but slippin' and slidin' through makes it even more fun!

MATERIALS

- Large plastic sheet (a 15-foot/5-m plastic tarp from the hardware store costs about $1, and lasts an afternoon)
- Soft, grassy area (a slight slope is best)
- Garden hose and sprinkler

LET'S DO IT!

When you've got your tarp ready, spread it out in a flat or slightly sloping part of your lawn. Hold down the four corners with smooth-edged rocks or large plastic bowls filled with water.

Set up your sprinkler so it "rains" on the tarp, making it slick. To use the slide, get a running start, and then slip and slide on your feet, tummy, or bottom.

P.S. If there are more than two of you playing, take turns to avoid crashing into each other, and watch out for any little tykes playing with you.

A POOL FULL OF GOOBLEK

Fill a kiddy pool with Gooblek and invite your friends over for a backyard bash. Hose down the mess when you're done!

Gooblek: Blend water and cornstarch in a ratio of 3 parts water to 5 parts cornstarch. Gooblek should be thick enough to form a ball by rolling it between your palms. Add more water or cornstarch, if needed. DO NOT EAT THIS!

Water Games

The great thing about water games is the more you lose (get hit with a water balloon), the more you win (get cooled off)!

Water balloon toss: Form two lines about 8 feet (1.5 m) apart. Spread out the players to double arm's length. Players on opposite sides gently toss water balloons back and forth, moving balloons down the line. See how many water balloons make it to the end. If a balloon breaks, enjoy the cool shower!

Water brigade: Provide each team with two buckets (one empty and the other filled halfway with water). Place the bucket with water at the goal line. The first player runs to the goal line carrying the empty bucket, pours the water from the half-filled bucket into the empty bucket, leaves the empty bucket, and carries the new half-filled bucket back to his or her team. The next player carries the water bucket, transfers the water, and returns with the empty bucket. Which team finishes first?

Visit the library . . .

Where are there plenty of silly ideas? Where can you explore the moon, take a trip around the world, go scuba diving, and escape to Narnia? Why, the library, that's where! Most libraries have summer programs just for kids like you — kids who want to have fun, discover new things, make special stuff, and go places. Sign up for a library card this summer with your own name on it. (Congratulations! That's *really* a treasure!)

P.S. If you can't read, you can still enjoy the books on tape, storytelling programs, and music sections, and you can still get a library card. If you want to learn how to read (or how to read better), talk to the librarian. He or she can get you some help, one, two, three. Yes, the library is a wonderful place, just waiting for YOU!

. . . out & about

Too Darn Hot!

When it's really hot outside, everyone gets a little bit irritable, everything feels sticky, and that banished phrase ("I'm bored!") creeps into your conversation. Oh, my! What to do?

897...

How about:

Making ice-cold lemonade (see page 9)

Sitting under a tree

Going to the park and watching people

Going to the library

Learning to whistle (see page 107)

Reading a book

Playing word games (see page 86)

Making a photo album (see page 104)

Lying on the grass and counting bugs or cloud-gazing

Having a cucumber-sandwich picnic (without the crust!)

Sketching a self-portrait (see page 91)

Cleaning out a toy box (and finding long-lost treasures)

Taking a bubble bath

Making a big salad for a cool dinner

Asking a grown-up to take you out for ice cream tonight

P.S. For more too-hot-to-do-anything ideas, see pages 90-120.

SODA FOUNTAIN COOLERS

The old-time soda fountain with high twirling stools and cool marble counters serving "brown cows," "chocolate malts," and "egg creams" is fast becoming just a memory from the "olden days" (back when your grandparents were kids), but kids of all ages still think ice cream and summer are one of the best combos ever. Here are some newly updated "old-time" treats!

Root beer float: This one is first because it's soooo good. Slowly add root beer to 2 scoops of low-fat vanilla ice cream or frozen yogurt. Stir ever so slightly so flavors will mix. Ice-cream floats can be made with any kind of soda — a "brown cow" is made with cola and vanilla ice cream. Try a float made with raspberry soda or 7-UP — it's delicious!

Chocolate ice-cream soda: Add chocolate milk to fill a third of a tall glass. Add 2 scoops of vanilla or chocolate low-fat ice cream or frozen yogurt, and fill to the top with seltzer water. Stir once or twice; then, top it off with whipped cream and a cherry. No soda fountain can do it better!

Milkshake: Blend 2 scoops of low-fat vanilla ice cream or frozen yogurt with chocolate milk for about 15 seconds.

Orange creamsicle: Blend until frothy and smooth: 1 cup (250 ml) very chilled orange juice, 1 scoop vanilla ice cream or frozen yogurt, and 7 ice cubes or chopped ice. Wow! Is this good!

make a difference

Make low-fat coolers.

Make these soda fountain treats out of nonfat frozen yogurt, skim milk, fat-free flavorings, and fresh fruit. Healthy, nonfat, and delicious! Make one for a grumbling grown-up who mistakenly thinks "nonfat" means "nongood."

CRITTERS, CRAWLIES, AND OTHER CREATURES

Summer is the best time to get up close and personal with all kinds of creatures, from the bugs bumping against your window at night to old Mr. Toad — "warts" and all! Shift your senses into high gear, crank up your imagination, and get ready to greet your neighbors (and a few unexpected roommates, too)!

INDOOR-OUTDOOR BUG HUNT

We humans sure are fascinated by bugs. From *Charlotte's Web* to *Miss Spider's Tea Party* to the movies *A Bug's Life* and *Antz*, people have been trying to figure out what these critters would be like if they had human feelings and behaviors. Why not go on a bug-hunting mission and see what you think "a bug's life" is really like?

WHERE THE CRITTERS LURK

We've searched out some of the favorite hangouts for these critters and crawlies. Many of them are hard to spot at first, due to their *camouflage*, or coloring, that blends with the natural scene.

Check it out: Search in the basement, the attic, the ground, and the base of trees and bushes for insects. Peek deep inside blooming flowers; check under leaves and plant stems. Turn over a rock to find crawling creatures. Look under loose bark for caterpillars. Don't forget to check under your bed (yup!), under the sink, behind radiators, around the windows, and high up in corners near the ceiling, too.

Bug-Hunting Supplies

◆ A keen eye
◆ Clean, clear containers with air holes or netting on top
◆ Trowel, or large spoon to collect specimens
◆ Notebook to write in and sketch the insects you find
◆ Banana and brown sugar (see Sugaring, page 26)
◆ A bug net (optional)
◆ Magnifying glass (optional)

For nighttime bug hunting:
◆ All of the above, plus a flashlight

Name That . . . 'er . . . Bug!

They creep. They crawl. They swim. They twirl, leap, and fly. They can walk upside down on the ceiling. Some even glow in the dark! Bugs are amazing creatures. And considering that there are about 1,000,000 of them for each person on Earth, you'd think we humans would know a lot about them.

Even though we usually call them all "bugs," there are actually differences among these creepy crawlies: There are *insects* like beetles, there are *spiders,* and there are *centipedes.* They are all related in a big group, or *phylum,* called Arthropoda, or arthropods. (Other arthropods are horseshoe crabs, lobsters, and shrimp.)

If it's an adult insect, you'll be able to see its three main body parts: head, thorax, and abdomen. The head will have two antennae, those threadlike sensors. The insect's six legs and one or two pairs of wings are attached to the thorax. And, the abdomen often has a pair of sensory organs called a *cercus* at its tip.

If you know it's an insect, but you don't know its name, ask yourself which major group it seems to fit in. Is it a beetle? A fly? A caterpillar? Give it a descriptive name you'll remember, like "leafy green dusk-flier with lacy wings."

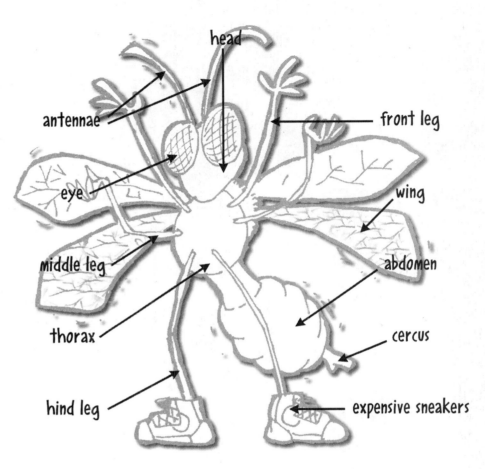

Don't Bug Me!

What makes a bug a bug? True "bugs" are insects that have a special beaklike tool for feeding and a special type of front wing. Not every insect is a bug. A ladybug is not really a bug — it's a beetle! And believe it or not, lightning bugs (fireflies) aren't really bugs *or* flies; they're beetles, too!

SUGARING

Here's a surefire way to attract bugs:

Mix an overripe banana with some brown sugar; let the mixture sit for a couple of hours. Then, slather the goo on the bark of a tree. Insects will soon appear, attracted by the scent of the sweet stuff.

You can sugar after dark, too. Put the goo out before dusk, and return with a flashlight after nightfall. Are there more bugs at the sugar now than there were during the day? Count the different kinds of arthropods (just about all those creepers and fliers) you've attracted. If you like to sketch — up close and personal — this is a good time, while they're occupied at the dessert buffet. One thing is for certain: Bugs seem to love sweets as much as humans do!

Do You Have Critter-Phobia?

If bugs give you the creeps, you're not alone. Many people share your feelings about these mighty strange little creatures.

If you're a shrieker or a "run-away-er," just remember this: Because of their silence, swiftness, and camouflage, bugs usually take us by surprise. But, if you *expect to see some bugs* when you are outdoors or in the basement, for example, they won't have that advantage of surprising you. In fact, it's more likely that you'll surprise them

Visit a natural history museum!

If creatures large and small are your thing, if you care a lot about habitats, if seeing a full-size dinosaur skeleton completely reconstructed would knock your socks off, you'll want to check out the nearest museum of natural history. The Smithsonian Institution has a listing of museums and field stations online at http://www.nmnh.si.edu/links.html. If you can't get to a museum, visit the American Museum of Natural History in New York City online (http://www.amnh.org) or The Field Museum in Chicago (http://www.fmnh.org).

MAKE A BUG HOTEL

Want to observe the insects you find? Simply invite them in from the wild for a short visit. You can keep them in a large jar — just be sure to punch lots of tiny holes in the lid. Or, you can easily make a more spacious bug house in a cardboard box with a screen or cheesecloth cover.

Keep your guests happy: Whatever the container, include some fresh, green leaves from the same kind of plant you found the critters on, as well as a little dirt, dead leaves, and a bottle cap full of water.

Don't borrow a creature for too long, though. Bugs have short lives and important environmental work to do. Please gently return your bugs to the exact place you found them after a few hours.

MUSIC! MUSIC! MUSIC! MUSIC! MUSIC! MUSIC! MUSIC! MUSIC! MUSIC! MUSIC! MUSIC!

When it comes to making music, Mother Nature is right up there with the best! Sit back, and enjoy one of the greatest orchestras around — for free! How many different sounds do you hear? How many "musicians" do you see skittering around? Look at the sky and at the ground. What a busy place!

MOTHER NATURE'S RECORDING STUDIO

How about getting some of that buzz from the great big world on tape? Borrow a camcorder, and head for the great outdoors to record dogs barking, birds chirping — any of nature's sounds. You and Ma Nature might just come up with some New Age (or would it be Old Age?) music!

How many different kinds of nature's music can you think of? Three? Five? Ten? Here's one to get you started — leaves rustling in the wind. Now, it's your turn!

... out & about

Summertime is concert time!

There's no doubt about it — outdoor concerts in summer can get to be habit-forming. Picture this: a nice picnic, a beautiful sunset, sitting on a blanket watching bugs in the grass, and then, just as night falls and the stars come out, the sweetest music imaginable. Attend a concert this summer, for sure!

THE SINGING WEATHERMEN

If you live near grass and trees, chances are you hear a chorus of chirping crickets each night. But, did you know you can calculate the approximate temperature in Fahrenheit degrees with cricket help? Count the chirps crickets make in 14 seconds, and add 42. The hotter the weather, the faster they sing!

SPINNING SPIDERS!

People either like them or they don't—spiders, that is! Some people run in the opposite direction, yelling "Get out of here!" Others quietly pick them up and place them safely outside. These are the people who know that, for the most part, spiders are helpful (they keep the bug population down), friendly, interesting creatures. Let's take a closer look and see if we can find new appreciation for these amazing spinners.

Spider at Work

Spider webs aren't really homes for spiders—they're actually traps for catching small insects to eat. It takes about an hour for a spider to spin a web (usually working at night). Look for one in the morning in the grass, garden, or next to the base of buildings. Don't disturb a web where a spider is working or where a fly has been caught—it might hold a spider's breakfast!

All done...

29

Strong as Steel

Few things seem more fragile than a spider web. Who would guess that pound for pound, a spider's silk is up to five times stronger than steel? Scientists discovered the silk's strength by testing its *tensile strength,* or the amount of stress it takes to make it tear.

PRESERVE A SPIDER WEB

If you're using black spray paint, choose white cardboard. If you're using hair spray, choose black paper. The contrast helps the web to show up better. If you want the strands of the web to really stand out, sprinkle them first with talcum powder.

MATERIALS

- ▼ A 6-inch by 6-inch (15-cm by 15-cm) piece of stiff paper or cardboard, black or white
- ▼ Black spray paint or non-aerosol hair spray
- ▼ Cardboard box
- ▼ Talcum powder (optional)

LET'S DO IT!

1. Place the paper in a box before spraying to protect the area around you. Working quickly (the spray needs to be slightly tacky), gently spray the web from both sides.

2. Then, hold the paper behind the web. Pinch off the web's guylines (where it's fastened), so the web rests on the paper. The wet spray will act like glue.

3. Later, spray the paper with a protective coating. To make a frame, glue some braided grass around the edge. You and a spider — nature's artists at their best!

BATTY OVER BATS

Let's face it: Bats have a bad reputation. They definitely need a new image with a new advertising campaign. Interested?

HOW MANY MOSQUITOES?

Some numbers are so big that most of us can't imagine them. Let's help that bat image with this reality check. Ask permission to pour a box of elbow macaroni into a large glass container. These are your "mosquitoes." Now, ask those around you to each guess how many "mosquitoes" are in your jar. Then, count them (put them in piles of 50 each). Who guessed the closest? Are there more or fewer than the 600 mosquitoes a bat eats each hour? Bats sure are busy keeping us mosquito-bite free!

Bat Saves Child from Hundreds of Bites!

The truth is that if you were a bat, you'd munch about 10 mosquitoes every minute! Now, one Texas bat cave houses about 25,000,00—that's *25 million*—bats. Together, they eat 500,000 pounds of insects each night. Just imagine how many insect bites we'd each have if there were no bats dining out every evening. Why, we'd have to take baths in bug spray!

GO ON A SWOOP SNOOP

To observe these insect-eaters at work, take a walk at dusk. Stand still and watch above you for flying bats. Although they like to dip and swoop, don't be alarmed. Despite rumors to the contrary, bats don't fly into your hair. In fact, they have no interest in you whatsoever. They're much too busy—well, you know—*munch, crunch, munch, crunch . . .*

To get to know these super bug-eaters better, contact Bat Conservation International, P.O. Box 162603, Austin, TX 78716 (phone 512/327-9721, or online at http://www.batcon.org). The more you learn about bats, the more you'll like having them "hanging" around!

WRITE A BAT-FOMERCIAL!

Here's the situation: Ms. Beatrice Bat is running for President of Nature Land against the incumbent and hard-to-beat Mr. Eddie Earthworm (nice guy), the always impressive Sir Bruce Bear (a bit stuffy), and that very popular Mademoiselle Honey Bee (young and very smart!). It's a tight race, a woman has never been elected president, and there are rumors spreading about Ms. Bat — how she frightens the neighboring humans and is constantly flying into things.

★ **Write a bat-fomercial** to be run on all the networks. Show what Ms. Bat has quietly accomplished all these years, and turn Ms. Bat into President Bat!

P.S. Not into writing? Draw a campaign poster showing Ms. Bat at her best!

EATS 600 MOSQUITOES IN 1 HOUR !!

BEATRICE BAT

FOR PRESIDENT

RADAR GAME

No matter what they say about Beatrice, bats are not blind. They use their *echolocation,* as well as their eyesight, to locate food and avoid anything in their paths. (Echolocation is the echo that bounces back to them when their squeaks hit an object.)

Here's the game: Play with your friends in an open field. Blindfold one bat "It." He or she listens to the other bats "squeak," and then tries to tag one of them. The "squeakers" can't move and must squeak constantly once the game begins. Last bat tagged is "It."

summer reads

Believe it or not, bats — which are *mammals* like us — are more closely related to you than they are to birds! A good "batty" read is *The Bat-Poet* by Randall Jarrell. Read *Stellaluna* by Janell Cannon, the story of a baby bat's journey to self-acceptance amid a nest of baby birds — an all-time favorite!

SQUEAK...

SQUEAK...

ROBIN?

NOPE! JUST A SPARROW.

MEET THE TOADS

Once you get to know these useful little creatures, you'll understand why "frog and toad are friends."

SAY "HELLO" TO A TREE TOAD

Toads seem to be just about everywhere—in fields, forests, gardens, yards, flowerpots, damp areas, and high mountainsides. By day, they often hide in cool, shady places, and then they come out at night. Look for little tree toads around mossy trees and under moist leaves. Invite one in for a short afternoon visit in your toad playground. After a few hours, please return it to its home. That's where it needs to be to live.

MAKE A TOAD PLAYGROUND

Set up a playground for your moisture-loving toad friends. A cardboard box lined with some recycled plastic bags works well. Dig up some soil along with some moss and grass. Put in some large stones and twigs for the toads to play on. Sprinkle water over your toad playground (and your toads, too) regularly. After playtime, return your toads to exactly where you found them, and invite them for another visit soon.

make a difference

Home, Sweet Home!

Yes, it is very tempting to keep tree toads overnight, bugs in your bug hotel, or hermit crabs on your trip home from the shore. *Please don't.* We're counting on you to make a difference. These are all very fragile critters, and they'll die if removed for long from their natural home, no matter how hard you try to keep them alive. Thanks! We knew we could count on you to do the right thing.

Toad True or False?

Touching a toad will give you warts.

Absolutely false! Those so-called warts are actually glands, or sacs, that give off a mild poison, making toads taste bad to cats, dogs, and other toad enemies, or predators. Pick up a toad, and we guarantee — no warts.

When you pick up a toad, it might urinate on your hand.

False. That wetness is pure water keeping the toad's body constantly moist. It could be a defense mechanism, too. Did it scare you enough so you put down the toad? Guess it works!

Toads bring bad luck.

False. We don't understand why toads have had such a bad rap; they're quite handsome creatures — and incredibly useful, too! If you're living where there are lots of mosquitoes, you should feel lucky if you have a toad living in a nearby flowerpot.

WRITE A "GOOD TOAD" FAIRY TALE

You can probably think of a lot of fairy tales where the toad or frog is cast as the unlovable character.

Here's your chance to write or tape record a story in which the toad is the hero, because toads really *are* wonderful characters. Perhaps your toad will rescue some children with its sticky tongue. Yes, the toad can be quite noble and wonderful when *you* are the storyteller!

Toad or frog?

How can you tell a toad from a frog?

FROG	TOAD
Smooth, slightly moist skin	Rough, warty-looking, dry-to-the-touch skin
Long legs, good for longer leaps	Short legs, good for short hops
Lives in or near water	Adults live on land
Lays eggs in strands in water	Lays eggs on land in clumps
Tadpoles are brown	Tadpoles are black

summer reads

Frogs and toads may be quite different, but that doesn't keep them from being best friends. Check out the stories in *Frog and Toad Are Friends* by Arnold Lobel. And, don't miss Kenneth Grahame's classic, *The Wind in the Willows.*

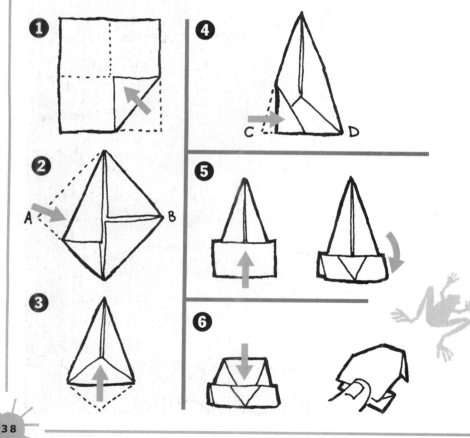

HOPPING TOADS

This little jumper is made from a 6-inch-square (15-cm) piece of paper. Leftover gift wrap or paper from a telephone book works well.

1. Place the paper, wrong side up, on the table. Fold it in half, first one way and then the other. Then, fold each corner to the center.

2. Fold points A and B, so they meet in the middle.

3. Fold the bottom up.

4. Fold C and D in, so they meet in the middle at the bottom.

5. Fold the bottom up, about one-third of the way. Now, fold this piece down in half again.

6. Fold the top point down. Turn over and press your finger down on the toad's back. Slide your finger off and watch your toad hop away!

NATIVE AMERICAN NATURE COUNT

School's out, your friends are away, and there's no one around. Or is there? What about the wildlife you share your habitat—the place where you live—with? Get to know the wild neighbors in your backyard or on your city block this summer by taking a nature count.

squirrel

raccoon

deer

wolf

bear

I Spy . . .

Wrens, sparrows, squirrels, pigeons, chipmunks, snails, moles, raccoons, rats, butterflies, mice, bees, bats, and rabbits are just a few of the wild creatures that often live close by. Since wild creatures are naturally camouflaged by Mother Nature, they're often much closer than you imagine.

Think like a detective. Did you see animal tracks in the moist mud? Paw prints on the sidewalk? Has your garbage been tipped over during the night? A raccoon might be on the premises. Or, does your nose tell you a skunk lives nearby?

Walk around the trees. Are there nests overhead? Are there small holes by the roots? Droppings or feathers on the ground? Pellets on the ground could mean an owl is nearby.

Look out your window and visit your backyard (or city balcony) at odd times of day. Jot down your findings for your nature count.

KEEPING HABITAT RECORDS

The first Americans kept count of what was important to them by marking hides and bark with feather pens and homemade dyes. Make a count of the animal life that shares your habitat in summer in the Native American way.

Make the "skin": Tear a brown grocery bag in the shape of a hide by cutting the bag apart at the seams, and smoothing it flat. Tear all the edges away, giving the bag a rough shape, like an animal skin.

Keeping track: Design symbols for each kind of wildlife you see. Each time you see a critter, mark a single line next to its symbol. Mark the dates you begin and end your count. Store your count by rolling it up and tying it with a piece of string, dried cornhusk, or yarn.

HERE COMES THE SUN

It's summertime, summertime, sum, sum, summertime! Big Old Mister Sun is smiling, showering us with rays filled with warmth and long stretches of daylight. We hope you'll be smiling, too, as you enjoy all that the summer sun has to offer!

WAKE UP, YOU SLEEPYHEAD!

You may think waking up early is for the birds, but early summer mornings are truly a breath of fresh air, no matter where you live. Plan an early morning of fun, food, and nature's glistening picture show—and start your day with the birds!

Breakfast Sundae

This is so good that you'll think you're having dessert instead of breakfast (and it's good for you, too)! Scoop low-fat yogurt into a sundae dish, layer on three kinds of fruit (like berries, bananas, and peaches), add a handful of cereal, and sprinkle with raisins. Top of the mornin' to you!

summer reads

While you wait for the sun to begin its majestic rise, read aloud from Barbara Berger's *When the Sun Rose*, Michael Emberley's *Welcome Back Sun*, or Byrd Baylor's *The Way to Start a Day*.

SUNRISE SILHOUETTES

Buildings and trees *silhouetted*, or outlined, against a gentle sunrise remind us of nature's beauty within a busy city or on a bustling farm — washes of muted color rising out of the night's darkness. Your sunrise silhouettes are a lasting treasure for those darker winter mornings to come.

MATERIALS

✳ Pink, rose, blue, purple, orange tempera

✳ Construction paper:

　　12 inches by 18 inches (30 cm by 45 cm), pale yellow, light blue, or cream

　　3 inches by 12 inches (7.5 cm by 30 cm), 6 black or dark blue

✳ Sponge, scissors, glue

LET'S DO IT!

1. Mix 1 tablespoon (15 ml) of tempera with 2 tablespoons (25 ml) of water (for each color). With a sponge, streak the tempera across the background paper. Introduce the colors that capture your impression of sunrise — muted, or glowing, or fiery before a sizzling day. Let dry.

2. Cut silhouettes — a cityscape of buildings, a forest of treetops, boats in a harbor — from the dark paper strips. Cut several windows or branch separations that let the "sunlight" shine through the buildings or the treetops.

3. Glue the strips beginning at the bottom edge of the paint-streaked paper.

PAINT THE SUNRISE!

With dew on the ground, and perhaps a rising mist in the air, the world seems to sparkle just as the sun breaks through. Use these home-made sparkle paints to capture that magical moment.

To make sparkle paints: Mix equal parts of flour, water, and salt. Pour some of the mixture into squeeze bottles or another container. Add tempera paint to each container and mix well. Squeeze or brush the paint onto paper, creating a design, impression, or picture. (When the paint dries, the salt causes the paint to sparkle.)

FLOPPY SUN HATS

Recycle the Sunday paper's "funnies" into stylin' sun hats — and don't be surprised if people stop you on the street to get the news!

MATERIALS

✴ 2 to 3 sheets of newspaper (full size)
✴ Masking tape, at least 1 inch (2.5 cm) wide
✴ Scissors
✴ Stapler
✴ Decorations

LET'S DO IT!

1. Layer the unfolded sheets of newspaper atop one another, and place them over your head, completely covering your face and the back of your head. Hold them in place around your neck.
2. Ask a partner to wrap masking tape (somewhat tightly) several times around your newspaper-covered head, just above your eyebrows.
3. Remove the newspaper from your head. Trim the corners, designing your hat to suit you. (You can staple or tape the edges together, or roll up the brim and tape, if you like.)
4. Decorate your hat with ribbons, baseball cards, tiny objects, junk jewelry, vines, flowers. To sponge stencils, see page 76.

Sun Sense

Hats, caps, visors, sun specs—they're all the rage now. And, they keep those midday rays (from 10 AM to 2 PM) off your head and away from your eyes and skin. The damage you do with sunburn today will come back to haunt you in the future. So, slather on sunscreen (with at least SPF #15), and put on that head and eye gear! Cool!

SUN BANNER

Create a sunshiny-bright banner by cutting a large rectangle from felt for a background. Fold down and glue or staple the top edge to create a slot for a dowel or straight stick. Glue on different-colored sun shapes cut from colorful felt or fabric scraps. Let dry; then, insert the dowel through the slot and hang with string from each end.

JAMMIN'

Fresh-picked strawberries announce the arrival of summer's fruity delights. Here's your chance to capture that once-a-year flavor in a jar, because summertime is berry time!

Visit a pick-your-own farm.

Head for a local pick-your-own farm to harvest strawberries at their sun-ripened peak. You pick the berries and then pay either by the pound or by the pint or quart. Pick enough berries so that you can make some jam, enjoy some strawberry shortcake, and still have plenty to eat straight out of the basket. To find pick-your-own farms near you, check under "Farms" in the Yellow Pages of the telephone book, call the Extension Service at your state university, or ask at local garden shops. Many places don't mind if you nibble some berries while you pick — one for the basket, one for me, two for the basket, one for me, three for the basket . . . !

... out & about

EASY REFRIGERATOR STRAWBERRY JAM

Buy these ingredients before you head for the berry farm, and while you're at it, pick up some Bisquick, eggs, and whipped cream for strawberry shortcake. Yum!

INGREDIENTS

- 2 quarts (2 L) strawberries, hulled and washed
- 1 package (1.75 oz/49 g) powdered fruit pectin
- Sugar (check pectin package for exact amount)

LET'S DO IT!

1. Crush strawberries in a large bowl, 1 cup (250 ml) at a time, using a fork or a potato masher. Measure out the exact amount of crushed fruit needed according to the pectin package directions, and place in a second bowl.

2. Measure sugar into a medium bowl (use exact amount specified on the pectin package).

3. In a small bowl, mix ¼ cup (50 ml) sugar from measured amount with powdered pectin. Stir sugar-pectin mixture into prepared fruit. Let stand for 30 minutes, stirring occasionally. (Eat those extra berries while you wait!)

4. Stir remaining sugar into fruit, stirring constantly until sugar is dissolved, about 3 minutes.

5. Pour jam into clean jars, leaving ½ inch (1 cm) space at the top. Cover. Let stand at room temperature for 24 hours to set. Refrigerate.

NOTE: This jam will stay fresh in your refrigerator for one to two weeks. For longer storage, store the jars in the freezer.

Makes 6 cups (1.5 L)

JAM JAR LABELS

For additional pizzazz, design your own labels. Who knows? Jam in summer, zucchini bread at harvest, applesauce in fall, and fudge in winter — you could be in business year-round! We know someone who made a business of selling her apple pies, so why not you?

Design-a-label: On paper or a computer, draw a shape for your label and write the name of your product, as in "Jason's Jams." Print out or copy as many labels as you need (save the master document).

When your jars of jam have cooled, wipe them clean and glue on the labels.

Cut a circle from scrap fabric large enough to cover the lid and neck of the jar. Attach with a ribbon around the jar. Very nice, indeed!

For You Mom...

STRAWBERRY
Jam

summer reads

Is all this picking, and eating, and planning making you tired? Treat yourself, and any younger kids around, to John Vernon Lord's storybook *The Giant Jam Sandwich*. Or, read *Blueberries for Sal* by Robert McCloskey.

make a difference

The ants come marching one by one . . .

Boo-hoo. Yup, it's the sad truth: When you cook, you (or a *pre*-designated helper) cleans. And in the summer, cleaning up means "de-sticking" all the counters, too. If you read *The Giant Jam Sandwich* (above), you'll know why. Those critters must have "sweets radar," and they're probably calling all their friends to head over to your house right now. So, put on some tunes, chatter with some friends, and get cleaning!

FRESH STRAWBERRY TOPPING

Slicing fresh strawberries for a wonderful topping is about the best thing you can do for a bowl of vanilla ice cream, yogurt, or cake — and don't forget pancakes, waffles, and French toast! Or, enjoy a bowlful of sliced berries in their natural juices. Slice half the berries and mash slightly; then, sprinkle with a bit of sugar, and add more sliced berries. Now *that's* what summer is all about!

RAISED PRETZEL RAYS

Who doesn't love fresh-baked pretzels? Warm, salted (or not), dipped in mustard, salsa, or spaghetti sauce—however you like them, they're delicious, and lots of fun to make, too. Bake a batch in recognition of the summer sun.

INGREDIENTS

1 packet active dry yeast
1 cup (250 ml) lukewarm water
2 tablespoons (25 ml) soft butter or margarine
1 tablespoon (15 ml) sugar
$^1/_2$ teaspoon (2 ml) table salt
3 to $3^1/_2$ cups (750 to 875 ml) all-purpose flour
TOPPING: 1 egg, water, coarse salt

LET'S DO IT!

1. Stir to dissolve the yeast in water. Add the butter, sugar, table salt, and $1^1/_2$ cups (375 ml) of the flour. Mix until well blended.
2. Stir in the remaining flour. Turn out the dough onto a floured surface; knead (push and pull) for about 5 minutes, until it is smooth and elastic. Put the dough in a greased bowl, cover with a clean kitchen towel, and place in a warm spot for about an hour, until the dough has doubled in size.
3. Punch down the dough and knead briefly. Divide into 12 pieces. Roll each piece into a rope about 1 inch (2.5 cm) in diameter. Form the ropes into pretzel shapes or twists, or form lengths into sun shapes with rays. (Brush the dough ends with water to help them stick.) Place dough shapes on a lightly oiled baking sheet. Cover with a towel, and let rise for 30 minutes.

4. Preheat oven to 450°F (230°C). Mix the egg with a spoonful of water and brush onto the pretzels. Sprinkle with coarse salt. Bake for about 12 minutes, until lightly browned. Let them cool down; then, eat 'em up!

Makes a dozen 6-inch (15-cm) knotted pretzels

Pretzel Lore

The knotted loop shape of the pretzel is a very old symbol, believed to have once represented the seasonal journey of the sun. (This was before people understood that the earth moves around the sun, and not the other way around!)

SUNNY SIDE UP

Well, it's not spelled "sunnertime," but the sun does figure in many English words and phrases, from Sunday to sunlight. Use "sun" words, phrases, song titles, and book titles to play a fun game of charades, silently acting out the words for others to guess. Here are some words and phrases to get you started. What other words can you add to the list?

RAIN, RAIN, STAY TODAY!

Who said rain spoils a summer day? We think that sometimes rain makes a perfect summer day — perfect for sending secret messages, reading stories aloud to yourself (and anyone else who wants to listen), baking a cake, going on a rainy-day walk, designing T-shirts "by you," and, well, lots of other fun things, as you'll see here. Rain in the forecast? Pick your pleasure and have a really glorious *rainy* day!

A WALK IN THE RAIN

Oh, yes, this is the greatest! Just put on your swimsuit to enjoy a let-the-gentle-rain-drip-down-your-nose-splash-in-the-mud-puddles-skip-twirl-and-catch-a-raindrop-on-your-tongue walk!

Critter sightings

No doubt about it! Most of nature is as excited about a gentle rain as you are. Look all about to see the earthworms that have come above ground for a refreshing shower, the frogs and toads that just love a rainy day, and, of course, the birds that like splashing in puddles as much as you do!

MAKE A HOMEMADE RAIN GAUGE

Does more water fall in a gentle, steady rain or in a sudden downpour? Take a guess, and then test to find out! Use a wide-mouthed container to collect the rain. Place a wide funnel inside it to keep the water from evaporating before you measure its depth.

Take measurements: Whenever it rains, collect the rainwater in the big container, but transfer it to a measuring cup to see how much rain fell. Then, in a summer rain log (post one on your refrigerator), write the date and how much rain fell. Note the approximate length of time it rained, and how hard it rained (gentle or downpour). Now, let your rain log *tell* you the secrets of rainfall. Are you surprised by what you learn?

Weather Warnings

Ever notice how animals seem to know when it will rain? Lots of weather sayings comment on the behavior of animals and nature. Maybe you've heard some of these.

If bees stay at home,
Rain will soon come.
If they fly away,
Fine will be the day.

Red skies at morning
Sailors, take warning
Red skies at night
Sailors' delight

Flies will swarm
Before a storm.

These sayings, even though they aren't scientifically accurate, have become part of our folklore. What do your pets do before a summer storm? (Does your dog hide under your bed before a thunderstorm?) How do you know when the weather is about to change?

Make up some weather sayings that you notice to usually be true. Here's one to get *you* predicting:

Leg aches by noon
Showers come soon.

summer reads

Who said rain and good times can't go together? Read *Just a Rainy Day* by Mercer Mayer, *Planting a Rainbow* by Lois Ehlert, and *Bringing the Rain to Kapiti Plain* by Verna Aardema for some rainy-day inspiration.

PITTER-PATTER PICTURES

Let gentle raindrops help you paint a picture! Paint some shapes or color splotches with water-soluble paints (such as watercolors or tempera paints) or markers. Place the painted paper outdoors in a gentle rain until the colors begin to run. Then, bring the painting indoors and quickly hold it at different angles to let the colors run as you like (this is where *your* talent comes in). Name your painting something descriptive or funny like *Rain in the Park* by ZJW and *Raindrop #3,537,641!*

YAKETY, YAKETY, YAK!

BLa BLa...

Just how many ways are there to communicate? We blurted out five ways right off. How many can you count? In these days of e-mail and instant replay (there are two), let's discover (or rediscover) together just a few wondrous ways to yakety, yakety, yak!

LEARN ASL

The hand language of the deaf, called American Sign Language (ASL), is fun to learn, beautiful to listen to, and, most important, by learning to *sign* (as speaking in ASL is called), you'll be able to speak with many hearing-impaired and deaf people.

ASL has individual letters of the alphabet for spelling out words (practice spelling your name), and some gestures and signs for whole words and expressions. We have illustrated here and on page 58 the signs for each letter of the alphabet, as well as for some frequently used words and expressions.

When first meeting a deaf or hearing-impaired person, ask if he or she prefers ASL, lip-reading, or both. If speaking with someone who lip-reads, be certain to speak clearly (but don't yell!), not too fast, facing the person, with your mouth uncovered. Then, chatter away!

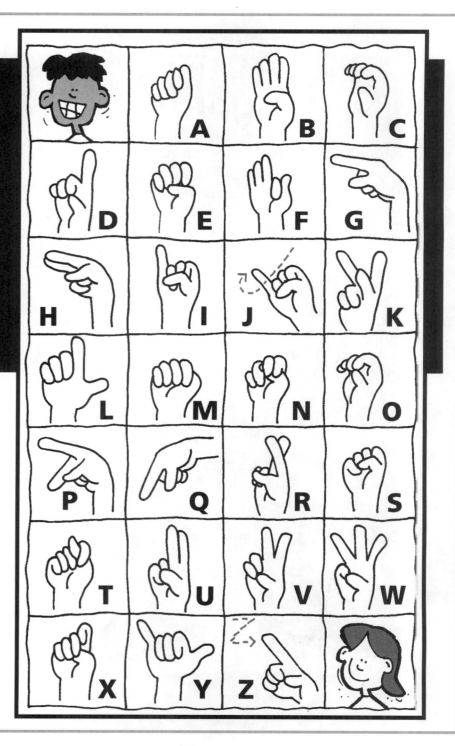

National Theater of the Deaf

This theater company puts on performances of modern and classic plays, all in ASL. The company sometimes tours North America, so you may be able to catch one of its performances. For more information: National Theater of the Deaf, P.O. Box 659, Chester, CT 06412. 860/526-4971; 860/526-4974 (TDD for the hearing impaired).

... out & about

Body Language

Do you ever feel that you are getting "mixed messages"? Someone says one thing such as, "Everything is fine!" but somehow you get the feeling everything is *not* fine.

That mixed message comes largely from body language—loud and clear communication from a person's arms, hands, stance, eyebrows, or mouth. *Watch* closely to *hear* the complete message!

make a difference

Good for all!

Learning to sign is a great first step, but don't stop there. Be sure to ask groups in your town or city to provide appropriate access for the hearing-impaired. Getting someone to sign at school events, for example, would be a good place to start.

"Speaking" with Signs

Body language is a big part of ASL, too. ASL uses familiar gestures — such as shaking your head up and down for "yes" and sideways for "no." The sign for "I understand" is the same as for "I don't understand." The difference is the look on your face when you make the sign!

Some American Sign Language is taken from the everyday movements you already make. For instance, to say "I," simply point to yourself. To say "you," point to the person you're signing to.

Try these simple phrases in sign language. How many different things can you say?

I

mother

father

please

I   love   my   wonderful   dog.

name   you   I love you.   finished

MAKE YOUR NAME SIGN

It's true that you can learn to sign your name very quickly, and that is a good way to introduce yourself in ASL. But, when you sign with your friends (and new acquaintances, too), name signs tell a lot about *you*. A name sign is like a nickname that describes you the way you think of yourself. Or, in some cases, it describes how others think of you. Deaf children, for instance, are often given name signs by their parents. Making a smile or touching the heart (like Ari's name sign, below) are two common name signs given from birth.

Thank you, Ari DiMaio, for introducing us to name signs.

There are many ways to make a name sign. One method is to choose a motion showing something you like to do (shooting baskets or reading a book, for instance). Then add a sign for the first letter of your first name to make the name sign yourts. What is your name sign going to be?

ARI
sign for A +
touches his heart

ERIN
sign for E +
open book made
with hands

RICKY
sign for R +
shooting a basketball

Want to Learn More?

Visit the website dww.deafworldweb.org/asl/. Look in this site under the category "culture and language" and then go under "name signs." This site also has a dictionary of common words in ASL. Think how many more people you can talk with now that you know ASL!

MORSE CODE MESSAGES

It may be difficult to imagine, but not that long ago, communicating with someone hundreds of miles away was a lengthy (think Pony Express and ships on seas) process. Then, in the 1840s, American inventor Samuel Morse came up with a system of dots and dashes to stand for letters, numerals, and punctuation marks that could be clicked on a telegraph machine, sending messages in code, across wires, to great distances away. People still use Morse code today on shortwave radios, and you can use it, too—for sending secret messages!

- Tap a message to a friend using the International Morse code alphabet.
- Send a secret Morse code message by e-mail.
- Send a message on a sunny day, using a flashing mirror.
- Signal at night with a flashlight by passing your hand across the beam fast, then slow, to differentiate the dots from the dashes.

We won't tell you how handy this all can be (like when the "if I hear one more word from you kids" warning is announced), but take it from us, Samuel Morse was a great friend to kids, both then and now!

TAP TAP TAP

International Morse Code

A	·–	J	·–––	S	···
B	–···	K	–·–	T	–
C	–·–·	L	·–··	U	··–
D	–··	M	––	V	···–
E	·	N	–·	W	·––
F	··–·	O	–––	X	–··–
G	––·	P	·––·	Y	–·––
H	····	Q	––·–	Z	––··
I	··	R	·–·		
, (comma)	––··––			?	··––··

You may notice that the "e" has one dot and the "t" has one dash in Morse code. That's because these letters are used most often in English, so Samuel Morse made them the simplest signals to send.

Now, for some practice, decipher this message, and then try stumping your friends by e-mailing coded messages to them.

···· ··   –··–   ·–– ···· ·– –   ·– ·–· ·

–·–– ––– ··–   –·· ––– ·· –· –·   ·–– ––– ··––··

·–– ––– ··– ·–·· –··   –·–– ––– ··–

·–·· ·· –·– ·   –––   ··· ·––· · –· –··

– ···· ·   –· ·· –– ···· –   ·– –   –– –·––

···· ––– ··– ··· · ··––··

–·–– ––– ··– ·–·   ··–· ·–· ·· · –· –··

RAIN, RAIN, *STAY* TODAY!

AY-SAY HAT-WAY?

Have you and your friends ever tried speaking in pig Latin, that age-old language known to kids just about everywhere? Latin, as you may know, is a real, ancient language that is the root of many English words. Pig Latin, on the other hand, is only as real as you want to make it. Here are the simple rules:

 If a word begins with a consonant, move the first letter to the end and add ay. "Dog" would become "ogday."

 If a word begins with two consonants, move both to the end of the word and add ay. "Child" would become "ildchay."

 If a word begins with a vowel, add the word "way" at the end, as in, "Pig Latin is awesomeway."

And here is one extra rule you will thank us for: Some parents, teachers, and grandparents, too, used to speak and write in pig Latin, so be "orewarnedfay!"

BRING OUT THE BOWLS!

It's sticky out, the drizzle continues, you've watched the raindrops race down the windows, and well, you are just dreaming of something yummy to eat. Dream no more, because it is time for that universal favorite— ice cream!

*I scream,
you scream,
the whole world screams
for ice cream!*

But not everyone screams for the same flavors. In Mexico, people like avocado ice cream, and some folks even eat ice cream made of pork rinds! Mango, pineapple, coconut, and banana are hits in the Tropics. And, though coffee ice cream is popular in the Americas, have you ever tasted this Japanese favorite — tea ice cream?

So, invite lots of ice-cream lovers to join you. And, for a real ice-cream treat, read *Aldo Ice Cream* by Johanna Hurwitz.

AROUND-THE-WORLD ICE-CREAM SUNDAES

In honor of the world of ice cream, build some ice-cream sundaes to eat now or for dessert for the family. Cover a table with some butcher paper, plastic, or newspaper. Bring out pints of vanilla and other ice-cream flavors. Put the mix-ins, toppings, and garnishes into small bowls (see coconut bowls, page 120). Then, dig in and make sundaes from around the world!

The Mix-Ins, Toppings & Garnishes

Africa: peanuts, peanut butter

Africa, Caribbean, Thailand, and Polynesia: grated coconut

Brazil: Brazil nuts

Canada: warm maple syrup

Caribbean and Polynesia: pineapple chunks, bananas

China: Mandarin oranges

Denmark: crushed butter cookies

England: crushed toffee bars (or use Heath bars)

England, U.S.A.: whipped cream

Germany: crushed spice cookies

Italy: maraschino cherries

Mexico: chocolate sauce, ground cinnamon

Middle East: pistachio nuts

New Zealand: sliced kiwi

Scotland: butterscotch sauce

Switzerland: muesli

U.S.A.: chocolate chips, M&M's, crushed Oreo cookies

Why is it that just about everyone loves puppets? Maybe they like the idea of speaking in funny voices, or taking on different personalities, or of saying things through a puppet that they aren't quite comfortable saying themselves. Or, maybe puppets are just plain fun — and good company, too!

PLENTY OF PUPPETS

Search through your box of odds and ends, a button box, a "junk" drawer, and your recycling bins. You're sure to find just what you need to make a one-of-a-kind puppet creation. Here are some materials you might use for bodies, clothes, heads, faces, hair, and decorations:

buttons, scrap fabric and paper, paper towel tubes, twigs, Popsicle sticks, tongue depressors, newspapers, small paper bags, old socks, old gloves, yarn, curled paper strips, paper plates, moss, straw, wire, steel wool, old jewelry

Add some white craft glue, staples, needle and thread, tape, tempera paints, crayons, and markers. Now, let the puppet-making begin!

STICK PUPPETS

Use Popsicle sticks, paint-stirring sticks, or long twigs. Draw your puppets on paper or cardboard; decorate with markers or paint. Make hair, and glue or staple head to stick. For arms, place a stick across the body, and then make clothes.

SPOON PUPPETS
(PREVIOUS PAGE)

Paint a wooden spoon. Draw on a face. Glue on yarn hair. Glue fabric on handle.

SOCK PUPPETS

To create a working mouth, cut and fold cardboard in half. Insert into the sock's toe; then, glue it in place for a mouth.

BOX PUPPETS

Cut a small box in half on three sides. Cover with colored paper or paint. Add decorations.

CARDBOARD-TUBE PUPPETS

Look what you can create (and this is just the beginning)! You'll need a cardboard tube, a small paper bag, and newspaper.

RAIN, RAIN, *STAY* TODAY!

THE PERFORMANCE!

There are many ways to make a puppet show theater. All you need is a place to hide the puppeteer (that's *you!*), while the puppets perform. How about sitting behind a sofa and having the puppets act on top of the sofa's back? For an outdoor show, stretch a clothesline between two trees and hang a tablecloth to hide the puppeteers. Or, construct a puppet theater from a large cardboard box: Just cut out a window, hang a cloth for a curtain, and let the puppet show begin!

make a difference

Baby-sitting brainstorms!

Here's a way kids of all ages can enjoy puppets. Each person makes a puppet (tube or stick puppets with paper-plate heads are easiest). Then, you read or make up a story while the kids act it out with their puppets. Be sure to leave room for lots of silliness in your story!

SHADOW PLAY

Making these movable shadow puppets is a lot of fun. And, with these, you can put on an amazing puppet show!

cut out the various pieces
punch holes for fasteners

tape to wire coat hanger

MATERIALS

- ☙ Pencil
- ☙ Poster board, about 9 inches by 12 inches (22.5 cm by 30 cm), per puppet
- ☙ Scissors
- ☙ Craft knife (with supervision)
- ☙ Hole punch
- ☙ 4 paper fasteners per puppet
- ☙ 2 wire coat hangers per puppet
- ☙ Wire cutters
- ☙ Pliers
- ☙ Tape

LET'S DO IT!

1. Sketch the outline of your figure on the poster board. Make it large enough so that the shoulder and elbow joints are at least 1/2 inch (1 cm) wide.

2. Cut out the figure with scissors. Use the craft knife to cut out any interior sections, such as the eye, ear, and buttons of this figure.

3. Punch holes in the shoulders and elbows as shown. Fasten them together loosely with the paper fasteners. There should be a little "play," so that the joints can bend easily. Cut the ends of the paper fasteners with the wire cutters so they don't show when the arms are moved about.

4. Cut a wire coat hanger (snip off the bent hook completely) the length of the puppet plus 8 inches (20 cm). Bend it with the pliers to make it conform to the figure. Tape the wire in place with short pieces of tape.

SHADOW SCREEN

To get the best effect with your large-jointed figures, stretch a white sheet across a doorway. To hide the puppeteer, make a barrier out of cardboard or an overturned table. Place a lamp or powerful flashlight at puppet level, positioned on a table or pedestal far enough behind you so you have room to move the figures.

summer reads

Make some hand shadows to add to your characters (see page 87 for some ideas). Are you stumped over how to make a whinnying horse or a big bird? Read *Fun With Hand Shadows* by Sati Achath and Bala Chandran, and learn to make everything from a cud-chewing cow to a dancing elephant!

★ **TIP:** Make a stand to hold several puppets when you are putting on a show. Stick the body wires into a thick piece of Styrofoam, or drill some holes in a block of wood to stand the puppets in.

IT'S TEA TIME!

Sometimes on rainy summer days, the ground feels damp, and you feel a little chilly. Here's a great way to take the chill off—with a friend, a sister or brother, a grown-up, or a special teddy bear. A pot of tea and some homemade cookies make every day bright!

TEA FOR TWO

DID YOU WASH YOUR PAWS?

MATERIALS

- Small pretty tablecloth or place mat
- Flower or some pretty leaves in a vase or glass
- A teapot (if you have one)
- Two cups and saucers
- Cloth napkins, or color some paper ones
- 2 teaspoons
- 2 tea bags
- Slices of lemon
- Honey or sugar
- A little milk in a small pitcher
- Some special cookies you baked, like Thumbprint Cookies (see page 71)

LET'S DO IT!

1. Set up your tea table wherever you are. It can be on a table, on the floor—wherever it will work and where your guest will be comfortable.
2. Put some water on to boil. Meanwhile, set the table and put out the cookies, milk, lemon, and sugar or honey.
3. Place a tea bag in each cup or both in the teapot. Pour the boiling water over the bags. Let the bags sit, or steep, in the water about 2 minutes; remove them.
4. Now, serve the tea and pass the cookies!

NOTE: Please get help with boiling water. Thank you.

make a difference

Visit an elderly neighbor.

Can you imagine how happy an older neighbor who doesn't get out much would be if you brought a tea-for-two party right to his or her house? Call first and invite yourself over. Then, serve up your tea and cookies. Here are some tips to help make your visit go smoothly:

- Forget about yourself and your surroundings. Instead, look at the person who is talking.
- Look through some photo albums together. Talk about the pictures and who the people are.
- Ask older people to share summer memories from their childhoods. You might be amazed (and even envious) of all the cool things they did as kids!

THUMBPRINT COOKIES

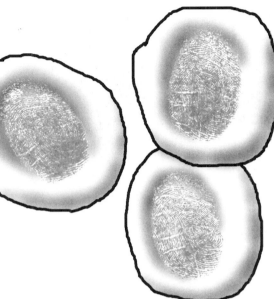

INGREDIENTS

2 cups (500 ml) all-purpose flour
1 cup (2 sticks) margarine, softened
½ cup (125 ml) sugar
2 egg yolks

For the filling:

1 jar of jam or preserves, or
chocolate kisses

LET'S DO IT!

1. Preheat oven to 350°F (180°C).
2. In a large bowl, mix the first four ingredients together until well blended.
3. Break off walnut-size pieces of dough and roll into balls. Flatten each ball in its center with your thumb and fill with jam or chocolate kisses.
4. Bake on a lightly greased cookie sheet for 25 minutes. Remove cookies to a wire rack to cool. Yumm!

Makes 36 melt-in-your-mouth cookies

Have a cool Fruit-Tea Party!

Too warm for hot tea? Make your tea and let it cool in the refrigerator while you are baking your cookies. To cool your tea more and sweeten it, stir in cold fruit juice. Add ice cubes. It'll be a happenin' tea party!

make a difference

A friendly ear...

You can help turn a bad day for a friend into a better one by giving your time and attention. It's as easy as 1, 2, 3!

1. Spend some time with someone who seems extra-quiet or sad.
2. Your friend may not want to talk, but don't be offended. Instead, just sit quietly together, listen to some music, or read a favorite story together.
3. Or, bring a board game to play with your friend—just the two of you.

71

FUN SUMMER SHIRTS

Turn a plain T-shirt into something special!

Six Quick Fixes

1. Paint or stencil a design with fabric paints.

2. Use an iron-on appliqué.

3. Sew ribbons or shoelaces on back with your initials or favorite team name.

4. Attach lace around the collar.

5. Paint racing stripes.

6. Sew patches out of neat fabrics.

TIE-DYE T-SHIRTS

Making dyed T-shirts requires some help from a grown-up, but you'll create a wearable work of art!

MATERIALS

- White, or light-colored, cotton T-shirt
- Package of hot-water dye
- Rubber bands
- Rubber gloves
- Plastic bag, 1-gallon (1-L) size

LET'S DO IT!

1. Wash the shirt in warm, soapy water, whether new or old; rinse well.
2. Wring out the shirt and place on a plastic-covered table, or outdoors on ground. Smooth out the wrinkles and bumps.
3. Fold and tie the shirt to create patterns of your choice. Wherever you bind the fabric, no dye can penetrate. To make stripes, fold the shirt, hem to neckline, in inch-wide (2.5-cm) accordion folds (back and forth). Evenly space four rubber bands around the bundle to keep it in place.
4. Get a dye bath ready following the instructions on the package. Put on the rubber gloves to protect your hands. Dye the fabric; then, let dry partially. Cut away the bands to reveal the pattern you've created, and hang to complete drying.

73

MAKE A SUNBURST!

Make a shirt as sunny as summer itself! Start with the shirt flat. Pinch the fabric near the center of the shirt; lift up. Twist the shirt in a tight spiral; then, roll it into a doughnut shape.

Place a rubber band around the outside to hold it in place. Dribble dye on the top; turn over, and dribble on the other side. Let dry partially, and then, open to complete drying.

BY THE LIGHT OF THE MOON

What's so special about moonglow in the summer? Maybe it's that sweaty, tired, thirsty feeling after a wild game of hide-'n'-seek or flashlight tag at dusk. Maybe it's the way the moon turns a deeper gold as we move through summer. Maybe it's knowing we can stay up a little later because tomorrow is — yay! — another summer day. Whatever summer nights mean to you, here are some happenin' things to do by the light of that silvery moon!

A special thank you to Susan Milord, Avery Hart, and Paul Mantell for their contributions to this chapter.

MAKE A MOON LIGHT

You may not be able to capture the moon and harness its light, but you can have the next best thing with this fun lampshade decorated with crescent moons and stars.

MATERIALS

☾ Scissors

☾ Stiff paper, such as tagboard or index cards

☾ Masking tape

☾ Light-colored lampshade, made from paper or smooth fabric

☾ Acrylic paint

☾ Paper plate or yogurt lid for paint

☾ Small sponge, about 1 inch (2.5 cm) square

LET'S DO IT!

1. Cut 8 to 12 crescent moon and star shapes from stiff paper. Tape the shapes to the lampshade using rolled pieces of masking tape stuck to the backs of the cutouts.

2. Squirt some paint onto a paper plate. Add enough water so the paint is the consistency of thick cream. Dip the sponge in the paint, blotting off the excess. Dab around the shapes on the lampshade, using quick, light movements, or cover the whole shade with dabs.

3. When completely dry, remove the cutouts carefully. Put the shade back on the lamp. Let there be moonlight!

BAKE CRESCENT COOKIES

Start this cookie dough right before dinner, and you'll be munching on crescent moon cookies for a nighttime treat. Or, shape store-bought cookie dough into crescents.

INGREDIENTS

1 cup (250 ml) flour
½ cup (1 stick) butter or margarine
1 cup (250 ml) finely chopped raisins or pecans
2 tablespoons (25 ml) sugar
1 teaspoon (5 ml) vanilla
Pinch salt
Confectioners' sugar

LET'S DO IT!

1. Combine the first six ingredients, mixing well with your hands. Chill in the refrigerator for 30 minutes.
2. Shape walnut-sized pieces of dough into crescents. Place on ungreased baking sheets and bake in a preheated 375°F (190°C) oven for 15 to 20 minutes, until lightly browned.
3. Let stand for 1 minute before removing from the sheets. Cool for an additional 5 minutes; then, roll in confectioners' sugar.

Makes about 20 cookies

WATCH A METEOR SHOW!

Wow! Fireworks in August! Well, not quite, but meteor showers are just as exciting. Around August 10 to 13, stargazers stay up late to watch the Perseid meteor shower, nature's own form of fireworks. An average of 65 meteors light up the sky each hour as they move towards Earth. The best time for viewing is after midnight, but you'll see plenty earlier. Bake some crescent cookies, make a thermos of hot chocolate, and watch the show!

WAXING   **WANING**

Wax & Wane

The moon doesn't generate its own light, so we see only the portion that is lit by the sun. When there's a full moon, the sun is shining directly on the moon; at other times our Earth gets in the way, shadowing the moon so that only part of it is visible. When the moon is *waxing,* it's heading toward a full moon, or growing. When *waning,* it's headed toward a new moon, or receding.

TIP: If the crescent moon mimicks the shape of your cupped *left* hand when held to the sky, it's waning. If it mimicks your right hand, it's waxing. Way to remember? More people are right-handed; hence the moon (like the number of right-handed people) is growing.

MAKE A MOON PHASES FLIP BOOK

Summer nights—when you are outdoors and awake later—are the perfect time to take notice of the moon's changing shape. Try keeping track of it each night for 30 days (the moon's shape cycle takes $29\frac{1}{2}$ days), drawing its shape on a calendar (you can make one with 7 boxes across and 5 boxes down, labeling the first box as night #1).

While you wait for nature's changing moonscape to unfold, you can fast-forward with this flip book.

To make a flip book: Copy the 16 pictures shown on plain index cards (make your drawings slightly larger). Arrange the cards in order, starting with #1 on top. Add a cover picture of your own design. Staple the left-hand side of the cards together. Flip for a rapid-speed glimpse of the moon's changing face!

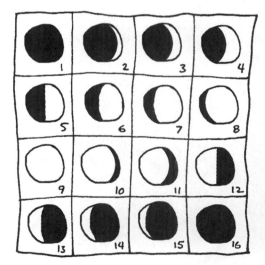

See a planetarium show!

Where can you go to see the night sky in the middle of a summer day? To a planetarium, that's where! Many museums have specially designed rooms where an exciting show about the stars and planets is staged. When the theater grows dark, and the music begins, you almost feel like you're traveling to worlds beyond our own. (Or, for an up-close look at the stars, visit an astronomy lab at a local college.)

WAX-RESIST NIGHTSCAPE

In wax-resist painting, the wax crayons resist the paint, so the crayons show through and only the bare spots absorb the paint. If you want your nightscape to be bathed in moonlight, use crayons in shades of yellow, gold, blues, purples, and white. Then, cover your whole drawing in black paint.

MATERIALS

◆ Medium-weight paper, about 9 inches by 12 inches (22.5 cm by 28 cm)
◆ Crayons in assorted colors
◆ Poster paint or watercolor (black)
◆ Large paintbrush

LET'S DO IT!

1. Draw an outdoor scene — city or country — or draw shapes like waves and ripples or branches of trees. Press down hard with your crayons. Create a mood with your colors — shimmering light, spooky shadows, or bright and festive.

2. Paint over the entire drawing in black. Let it dry.

ART TIP: Fluorescent crayons work well with this technique.

SERVE UP A SOLAR SYSTEM SUPPER

Surprise your friends or family with a summer solar system supper. Make a tablecloth out of a long piece of brown butcher paper: Draw a brightly colored sun at one end of the paper, and then draw and color each planet as suggested in the chart (these are the colors of the planets as they appear through powerful telescopes). This scale of relative distances is based on the distance from the earth to the sun equaling an inch (2.5 cm).

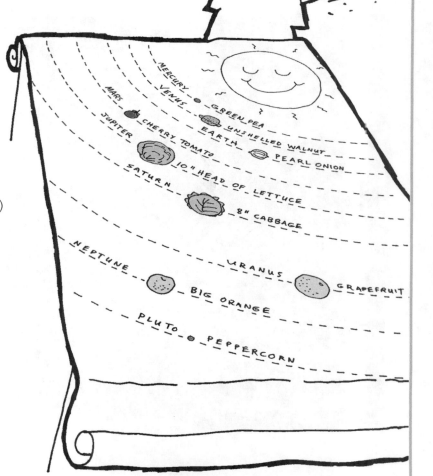

PLANET	DISTANCE FROM SUN (TO SCALE)	COLOR	RELATIVE SIZE
Mercury	2/5 inch (1 cm)	orange	green pea
Venus	3/4 inch (2 cm)	yellow	walnut in shell
Earth	1 inch (2.5 cm)	blue/brown/green	pearl onion
Mars	1½ inches (3.5 cm)	red	cherry tomato
Jupiter	5⅕ inches (13 cm)	yellow/red/brown	10-inch (25-cm) head lettuce
Saturn	9½ inches (24 cm)	yellow	8-inch (20-cm) cabbage
Uranus	19⅕ inches (48 cm)	green	grapefruit
Neptune	30 inches (75 cm)	blue	large orange
Pluto	39⅖ inches (98.5 cm)	yellow	peppercorn

NOTE: The sun, according to this scale (relative sizes), would be as big as a large house!

SUMMER FUN!

How about some **Planet Burgers** (burgers stuffed with a surprise chunk of "sun" cheese in the center), a **Solar System Salad**, and an **Eclipse Sundae** (scoop of ice cream darkened with hot fudge).

summer reads

The full moon is so bright you can almost read by its light — perfect for reading James Thurber's story, *Many Moons*, or the poems in *Thirteen Moons on Turtle's Back* by Joseph Bruchac. If folktales are more to your liking, check out Susan Milord's *Tales of the Shimmering Sky*.

Plant Some Moonbeams

The moonflower, one of the most fragrant flowers in the garden, stays tightly closed during the day, showing its huge blooms only at night! Each bloom lasts for only one night, but one plant has many blooms each night — and oh, they smell divine!

Moonflowers are easy to grow. If summers are short where you live, start seeds indoors 4 to 6 weeks before nighttime temperatures stay above 50°F (10°C). Because moonflowers don't like their roots disturbed, remove the root ball in one piece when settling your young plants outdoors. Make some sort of trellis with sticks and string for these vining plants to climb.

BACKYARD CAMPING ADVENTURE

Sleeping out under the starry sky in summer is pure magic! Put it on your "I-would-love-this" list— whether you live in the country or city.

TENT SHOULD FACE SOUTHEAST

MAKING CAMP

1. Pitch your tent on smooth, level ground, facing southeast to catch the first morning rays.
2. Use a tarp to cover the dining area and supplies.
3. If a campfire is in your plans, gather firewood while there's still daylight; stack it in a sheltered area. Or, use a camp stove.

NOTE: Make sure everything is secure from animals before turning in for the night. And, *really, truly, honestly* — don't bring food (or toothpaste) into your tent, or you'll be sharing your home-away-from-home with raccoons, bears, and skunks!

TENTING
Minus the Tent

No tent? No problem! One of the great things about backyard camping is that you don't need much of anything. With some blankets and perhaps a tarp or tablecloth, you'll be able to rig up a super tenting sight. Have fun!

city camping

Hey, city kids! There's lots of opportunities for summer camp-outs for you, too! A rooftop patio or garden will get you out under the stars, or call your recreation department or parks department to find out the location of the closest safe campground. Ask a grown-up to accompany you on your overnight camp-out adventure. Don't forget some bug spray and one flashlight per person. Leave the radio at home and listen to nature's cool sounds. Really awesome.

Need a sleeping bag? Here's one that will stay together all night. Just fold and pin a blanket like this, using giant-sized safety pins, facing the pins toward the outside of the blanket. Or, baste (large stitches) the blanket with strong thread or dental floss.

BY THE LIGHT OF THE MOON

Knots to Know

Every camper — backyard, wilderness, or living room — will want to know the ever-useful clove hitch and square knots. So, grab a rope or a length of strong twine to practice on.

*Use a **clove hitch** to attach guylines. You can tie ropes to trees with this knot, too.*

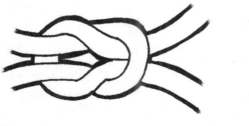

*The **square knot** is useful for tying up camping gear, tying ties, ribbons, and lots of other things.*

CHOW TIME!

Half the fun of sleeping out is camp food. Here's a camp-out menu that's easy and good. Don't forget your plates, cups, and utensils!

MENUS

Dinner
Dogs-in-a-blanket, bug juice, carrot sticks, walking fruit salad

Nighttime snack
S'mores

Breakfast
Biscuits-on-a-stick, fresh oranges

Where do you suppose the names bug juice, walking fruit salad, and s'mores come from?

Camp Cookin'

Save your sticks for dinner, snack, and breakfast.

Dogs-in-a-blanket: *Unroll the dough from store-bought crescent rolls. Wrap the dough around a hot dog, leaving both ends sticking out. Moisten the dough's edges with water and press together to seal. Put it on a stick and roast over hot coals, or bake in a 350°F (180°C) oven for 15 to 20 minutes.*

Bug juice: *Mix three kinds of juice in any proportion: grape, orange juice, cranberry-apple, or whatever flavors you like!*

Walking fruit salad: *Use an apple corer to carve out the center of an apple, fill with peanut butter, and top off with some raisins.*

S'mores: *What's a camp-out without s'mores? They're a North American tradition! Make a graham cracker sandwich filled with a piece of a milk chocolate bar, and a toasted marshmallow, cooked to perfection over the fire. Yum!*

Biscuits-on-a-stick: *Roll refrigerator dough for one biscuit into a "snake." Twist the raw biscuit snake around the end of the stick. Bake over the fire, turning often. When cooked, slide the biscuit off the stick and fill with jelly or butter. Mmmmm.*

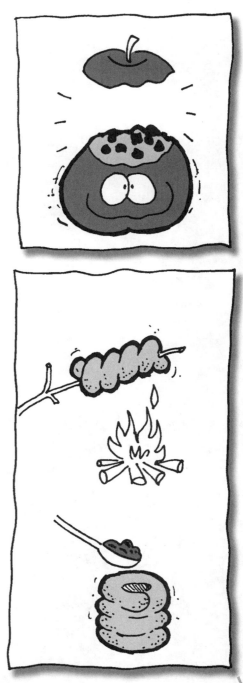

NIGHTTIME, FUNTIME

Whether sleeping under the stars, out by the growing pumpkin patch, on the balcony, or in the living room, here's some fun and funny stuff to play.

◆ **Tell spooky stories.** Ghost stories are great around the campfire or when you're snuggled in your sleeping bag, safe and sound. Take turns telling the spookiest story you can. Flashlights shining upwards under the story-tellers' chins are a must!

◆ **Play "Twenty Questions."** Someone thinks of some-thing—an object, an animal, a person, whatever. The other players ask questions about it until they can guess what the person is thinking of. The rules are that you may only ask questions that can be answered yes or no, and you are allowed only 20 questions altogether. Here are some good questions to start with:

> ★ *Is what you're thinking of alive?*
> ★ *Is it a plant?*
> ★ *Is it an animal?*
> ★ *Is it as big as a house?*
> ★ *Is it smaller than a car?*

If, after 20 questions, no one has guessed the answer, the person tells the group and then tries to stump everyone again. If the group guesses, the person who made the correct guess is the one to think of some-thing next.

◆ **Make hand shadows.**

Shadow a deer, a rabbit, a butterfly, and
more by simply shaping your hands in front of a flashlight someone
holds for you (see puppets, page 64). Can your friends guess what you are making?

◆ **Sing some rounds.** No one can sleep? Here's a way to stay in your tent and settle down,
sort of! When you sing a round, someone joins in at the right time, and the melody goes around
and around! Some good "round" songs are: "Frère Jacques (Are You Sleeping?)," "Make New
Friends," "White Coral Bells," and "Kookaburra." Perhaps the most famous round is "Row, Row,
Row Your Boat," a round with three parts. The second singer begins as the first gets to "gently
down the stream," and the third singer begins as the first sings "merrily, merrily, merrily, merrily."

P.S. The tricky part is sticking to what you're singing while your friends are singing
something else. Cover your ears!

◆ **Play "Grandma Is Strange."** Someone is the grandchild, thinking of a secret peculiarity of his or her *imaginary* grandma. The grandchild mentions one of grandma's strange likes and dislikes. For example, grandma loves tomatoes, but hates cake. And she's crazy for onions, but hates ice cream. The other players must guess the secret of her likes and dislikes. In this example, the grandma only liked words that had O in them. If one of the players guesses the combination, she can test out her idea. She might ask, "Does grandma love opera and hate rap?" First player to guess becomes the grandchild.

Grandma can love words with double letters, or things that are only one color, or creatures that fly — or, you name it!

◆ **Play "Moon-Star."** Who can name the most songs, books, and words with the words *moon* or *star* in them? Triple points if you name one with both words.

◆ **Catch a falling star.** Search the night sky for a shooting star. If you are patient, you are likely to see at least one, and some nights, you can see many.

Shhh...

Good Night!

Good night
Sleep tight
Don't let the bedbugs bite
But if they do
Squeeze them tight
And they won't bite tomorrow night!

The words to *Taps,* the quiet bugle call announcing bedtime, make a great finale to your evening camp-out. Sing them quietly and slowly.

Day is done;

Gone the sun

From the hill,

From the lake,

From the sky . . .

All is well;

Safely rest . . .

God is nigh.

make a difference

Breaking camp.

There is only one basic rule when breaking camp — no matter where you camp out! Leave the area cleaner than when you arrived. That means picking up all litter (and taking it out of the woods with you), filling any holes you may have dug, and, of course, putting your campfire completely out with both water and sand.

HELLO, SELF!

If you get to spend some time alone this summer, count yourself lucky. Most of us don't spend enough time with ourselves to know who we really are — what we think, what we like to do, what our own hopes and fears are (and what we are going to do about them). Here are some things to do when you are with the most important person in your life — YOU!

PICTURE PERFECT!

What better way to get to know yourself than to look in the mirror? Take a close look at yourself from the neck up. What is the shape of your head—oval, round, a square jawline? Did you discover anything new about yourself, like your long lashes above those sparkling peepers?

Now, pick your artistic medium (materials). Many portraits are done in chalk or charcoal, so the artist (that's you) can soften lines with smudges, use shading, and blend colors, but use what you have and whatever you like. Pick a textured creamy or pale color paper, if available.

Simple Secrets

Use these tips from the pros in portraiture!

Simple secret #1: Draw the *shapes* and *lines* that you see when you look in the mirror. Forget about a face, or a mouth and eyes; just draw triangles, ovals, lines, rectangles, and arches in relation to one another.

Simple secret #2: When drawing a kid-size head, divide it in two from the top of the head to the top of the eyebrows, and from the eyebrows to the bottom of the chin. Draw kids' eyes larger, and the nose and mouth slightly smaller than a grown-up's nose and mouth. (Your nose is about the same width as your eye, and your mouth is just a bit wider.)

Not Too Serious!

Does everyone know you for your wonderful smile? Your cool, spiky hair? For fun, exaggerate (overemphasize) certain features in your self-portrait, perhaps making your freckles enormous or your smile go from ear to ear. These exaggerated drawings, called *caricatures,* are often used in political cartoons in newspapers.

... out & about

Visit an art museum!

Art museums can be lots of fun, especially if you have a special mission. Visit a museum and ask at the information desk if there are any well-known self-portraits in the museum. Many artists, including Vincent Van Gogh, Rembrandt, Frida Kahlo, and Mary Cassatt, have painted self-portraits. Ask yourself: What did this artist think of himself or herself?

ALMOST-INSTANT SCULPTURE!

Turn a favorite photograph that focuses on one person or object into a free-standing piece of sculpture! This works best with an 8-inch by 10-inch (20-cm by 25-cm) photo, but you can enlarge one on a copy machine and use that, too. Glue it on foam-core board or a sturdy piece of cardboard. You'll need two pieces of wood molding, the size of the cutout's base.

To make a photo statue: Cut around the outline of the photo's subject. Glue the cutout to the foam board. Now, cut carefully with a craft knife around the photo. Leave a straight edge at the bottom. Then, paint or stain the wood molding. Glue the photo statue between the two strips of wood, forming a stand.

P.S. If you enjoy doing this, make several over the summer, and put them away for holiday gifts next winter. Just don't forget where they're hidden!

BEDROOM REVAMP!

On the one hand, you're lucky to have a room — even a shared room. On the other hand, year in and year out, it can get pretty boring staring at the same four walls and ceiling. Time for a change of scenery? Well, maybe you can get permission to paint a mural on your walls or a constellation on the ceiling, but don't count on it. Here are some more easily approved ideas that will go a long way to giving you a new point of view.

DON'T MOVE ANYTHING – YET!

Tired of waking up on the same side of the room every morning? Give your bedroom a whole new look— from grunge to totally awesome! You can use a computer drawing program to experiment with different designs. Or, draw a floor plan of your room on graph paper and cut out colored shapes for your furniture. (The view on a floor plan is as if you are looking down from above. Mark the windows, doors, and closet, and where the electric outlets are, too.) If you share a room with your brother or sister, you'll want to work on this revamp together.

Move the "furniture" shapes around until you get things arranged the way you want. Remember the key words — size, shape, proportion — because you want everything to fit.

Ask yourself: *Do I have a quiet place to read and study?*

Will I be able to read in bed at night?

Is there plenty of floor space to play?

If you love the new arrangement, double-check with the grown-ups, and start movin'!

MY MOST AWESOME ROOM

First, draw your room's floor plan.

Then draw the furniture.

BED

DESK

CHAIR

BOOKSHELVES

RUG

TRASH CAN

BEAN BAG CHAIR

Drag the furniture onto your floor plan.

WINDOW

WINDOW

CLOSET DOOR

DOOR

Room Revamp Tips

Having rearranged more than our share of rooms and having shared rooms with brothers, sisters, and roommates, we can speak from experience here. So, let us be so bold as to suggest:

◆ **Open your windows and shades.** Let the summer light indoors. Take a good, hard look—and notice what you like and what you don't like. Natural light gives your room a wonderful golden glow (and also shows the dust balls).

◆ **Get some orange crates** from the grocery store. Paint and stack them for great storage, display space for your favorite things, a place to keep clothes you never wear but can't give away yet, and as a bookcase. (Keep some crates empty to stuff things when your room is supposed to be clean.)

◆ **Odd-shaped rooms are super** even if you can barely stand up in them. Really. They have character (but usually no closets!), and nooks and crannies that have multiple uses — a place for your cat to sleep, forts, and secret hideaways. Pick a dark corner under the eaves and claim it as yours with a "Private! Keep Out!" sign. As long as apple cores aren't growing green stuff in there, people will respect your privacy. Add a big, squishy pillow, your favorite teddy and action figures, a treasured book, paper and markers, a flashlight, and even your baby blanket (everyone else still has one, so why not keep yours where you can enjoy it?).

◆ **Sharing a room?** Put two bookcases back-to-back between the beds for some private storing and snoring. Use the bookcase facing you for your night reading, favorite things you like to look at and fiddle with, an alarm clock, a clip-on lamp, and a CD/tape player. The last two are good investments of your baby-sitting and lawn-mowing money, because they keep peace in your room when one of you wants to read and the other wants to listen to music with the lights out.

HELLO, SELF!

DESIGNER CHIC

The key to making a room look put together, to making all your wonderful treasures and collections look like more than a pile of junk (how dare they say that?!), is simply grouping all similar treasures together.

Hang all your model airplanes in one area from different lengths of fish wire tacked to the ceiling. Collect all those pillows you love and pile them at the head of the bed, re-covering some in a piece of old velvet or an old floral print dress. Pile your stuffed animals in crates stacked up to the ceiling.

Whatever you collect — dead bugs, rocks, action figures, pictures of cool cars, bottle caps, weird buttons, horse pictures, animal miniatures, pieces of ribbon — group them all together on a shelf, hang them from wire or a mobile, or make a huge poster-board collage — and suddenly, you and your room will look just too cool. Without spending a dime!

Desk Organizer

Use a can opener to take off the ends of washed-out soup or juice cans. Cover any sharp edges with masking tape, then paint them — solid or a design — or glue on gift wrap. When the decorations are dry, fasten the cans together using latex epoxy glue (available at hardware stores) to create a pyramid of cans on their sides. Use clothespins to hold cans securely in place while the glue dries. Make a matching pencil holder from a single decorated can.

COOL CAP RACK

Read *Caps for Sale* by Esphyr Slobodkina (you are never too old), and then you'll know why you need to make one of these fun cap racks for your room. Leave it plain, paint your name, or stencil some designs on the rack.

P.S. You can do most of this yourself. It's a good way to see how easy it is to make useful things from wood.

GOOD SHOT!

MATERIALS

✿ Sandpaper
✿ 15 inches (37.5 cm) 1x6 pine board
✿ Oil-based or latex paint
✿ Pencil
✿ Drill (for grown-up use only)
✿ (4) 1-inch by 2⅛-inch (2.5-cm by 5-cm) Shaker pegs with a built-in wooden "tenon"
✿ White glue (like Elmer's)
✿ (2) 1⅛-inch (1-cm) screw eyes

LET'S DO IT!

1. Sand the board's edges.
2. Paint a background color on the rack. Let dry. Lightly mark where the pegs will go: 3 inches (7.5 cm) apart and 3 inches (7.5 cm) in from sides. Have a grown-up drill a ½-inch-diameter hole to fit the peg.
3. Sketch a design on the rack if you want; then, paint carefully. Paint pegs to match. Let dry.
4. Glue the ends of the pegs and tamp them in place. Screw eyes into top for hanging.

STRING AND YARN FUN!

Have you ever watched a kitten play with a ball of yarn? It's as if you had given it the greatest gift on Earth. We can't promise you the absolute in entertainment here, but for sure, you will be amused (and maybe confused) by the fun you can have with a simple piece of yarn. Go for it— and may the best cat win!

CAT'S-TAIL FINGER-KNITTING

All you need for this is a ball of yarn and your fingers! Use your creation for a bookmark, a bracelet, or if you get really ambitious, a belt or string tie.

1. Let about 6 inches (15 cm) of yarn dangle down the back of your hand between your thumb and index finger.
2. Wind the yarn over your index finger, under the next, over the ring finger, and under and around your pinkie.
3. Continue winding, going back under your ring finger, over your middle finger, and under and around your index finger. Repeat the whole sequence, index finger to pinkie and back again, once more. Now, pull the bottom loop on each finger over the top loop (and off your finger to the back side of your hand). You have knitted one row.
4. Repeat the winding pattern down to your pinkie and back again one time to make the next new row of loops. Then loop each bottom loop on each finger over the new top loop to make another knitted row.
5. Continue until the "snake" winding down the back of your hand is as long as you'd like it. Cut off the extra yarn and slip the end through the end loops so your knitting doesn't unravel.

make a difference

Whittle, knit, tie flies . . . with a "senior"!

Do you have an interest in knitting, tying fish flies, whittling, or some other old-time skill? Check in with the older experts in your life or at a nearby retirement community. Most elderly people would love to share their skills with the "younger generation"— you!

KNOT A KEY CHAIN

Summertime has always been a popular time to make key chains. Maybe that's because so many keys get lost when their owners are playing outdoors. Here's a great key chain to attach to a belt or backpack.

String keychain: Make a slipknot with a piece of cotton string or lanyard leather, as shown (A). Hold the loop in your left hand; with your right hand, pull a bit of free string up through the loop, pulling until a new knot forms next to the first knot (B). Pull the continuous string with your right hand, reducing the size of the new loop. Continue making new loops and knots until the cord is as long as you like. Cut the string and put the cut end through the last loop. Pull tight and knot. Slip your key on the cord and tie the ends together. Attach it to the inside of your backpack or your belt for an almost guaranteed, never-lose-again key chain.

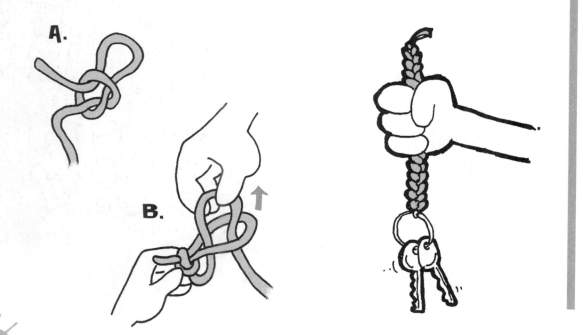

A.

B.

Well, get movin' and groovin' to that beat locked inside you! Who cares if you are the only one home—or, you are baby-sitting your little sibs. Get off the couch (yes, you, Mr. Couch Potato Head!). Head outdoors! Shake the willies out and bring on the sillies!

TAKE A MOON WALK!

Here's a dance step that will never go out of style. It got its name because you'll look as if you're defying gravity—skimming above the ground, moving in a very groovy way.

To moon walk: Bend your right knee and lift your right foot from the arch, sliding the foot backward. The left foot is raised as the right one seems to "land" in back of you. Actually, you adjust its position so that it's just under you. The second your right heel hits the ground, begin lifting the left foot, and vice versa, so both legs are always in a state of changing position. You'll appear to be slide-walking backwards!

Here's the secret: Make a super-smooth movement as you work both legs simultaneously. Hold your arms and head as if they were floating out from you. You don't travel very far in this dance. It's all a fun optical illusion.

Body Talk

Can you walk on tiptoe
As softly as a cat?
And can you stomp along the road
Stomp like that?
Can you take some great big strides
The way a giant can?
Or walk along so slowly
Like a poor bent old man?

Thank you, Avery Hart and Paul Mantell, for your moon-walking expertise and "Body Talk."

101

HELLO, SELF!

Attend a dance performance . . .

There are many summer opportunities to enjoy professional dance performances. Whether it's clogging, Irish dancers, flamenco, or a ballet company at its summer residence, see the art of dance this summer for a wonderful treat. Dancers can be strong and precise, and also beautifully graceful and expressive. It's almost magical!

... out & about

CALLING ALL SUPER-JOCKS, Male *and* female!

Calling all guys and gals! How would you feel about attending ballet classes this summer? Ballet dancers are in top physical condition: They have finely tuned bodies; they are very strong, very disciplined, and have excellent focus and concentration. And, they do long workouts every day. Just what *every* athlete needs. Call a local performing arts center or recreation center to see about enrolling, and speak with the teacher about your goals.

PRIVATE THOUGHTS

A photo album, sketchbook, or journal is a special place to record your most private thoughts, feelings, and how you see the world around you. It's where you can express exactly what you think and feel about your life, the lives of those around you, or the world at large. Best of all, you don't have to show it to other people. Start one this summer and see where it leads you. Let your inner humor, your insights, your sadness and gladness blossom in this private place.

P.S. If music is your form of self-expression, then write some music that captures your feelings—just as another person might sketch or draw. Hammer out a tune, bar by bar, as the thoughts and feelings flow.

JOURNALS, PHOTO ALBUMS, SKETCHBOOKS

Staples

KA-CHUNK!

Add cover design

Glue on strip to cover staples

Center fold

Marks for stitches

Stitch up center fold

Tie up ends

If the making of a book is exactly why you never keep one, then here's your answer. Just use an old notebook, sketch pad, or a stack of paper in a binder. It's *what* you record, not what you record it on, that counts.

But if the making of a book is part of the way you express, "This is about me!" then here are two easy ways.

A stapled book: This is the simplest book to make. Place the pages between two covers of your own design, and staple along the left side. Or, use a hole punch, and put in metal fasteners.

A hand-sewn book: Use thick paper and extra-strong thread or dental floss. The paper should be twice as long as you want each page to be. Be sure to put a piece of paper on for the cover, too, before you sew.

Put the pages together and fold them in half. Open the book, mark a straight line in the middle in neat dots about an inch (2.5 cm) apart, and sew along the lines.

summer reads

If you really want to know what someone's thoughts are about his or her life, then ask. And if that person isn't nearby or is someone famous whom you are curious about, maybe he or she wrote an *autobiography* (a book someone writes about his or her own life). Ask at the library or a bookstore for a book about or by someone who did something you are interested in. Try *Mark McGwire & Sammy Sosa* by Mark Stewart. Or, read the classic *Anne Frank: The Diary of a Young Girl* by Anne Frank.

GETTING STARTED

Hmmm! What's on my mind? What pictures flash across my eyes? What tunes are playing in my head? Grab a cool glass of juice fizzed with some soda water and fancied up with a slice of orange or lime. (Treat yourself *real* nice!)

Then, tuck these thoughts away:

★ There is no right or wrong in your book.

★ There is no good and bad.

★ There is no best or worst.

★ Real or imaginary—both are fine.

★ No one but you need ever see this.

★ This isn't school; it's personal time.

★ You are doing this for yourself.

★ It's a fun way to get to know yourself better.

We'll get you started:
Picture yourself sitting high up in a treetop. Now, write, sketch, and/or click away in a real or imagined way about how you feel way up there, and what you see way down here.

make a difference

Try a different point of view.

Sometimes, all of us get stuck thinking about people or ideas in only one way. We may have always thought the kid down the street is a "nerd," the older neighbor next door is "mean," or all people of a different race or religion are "no good."

Try a different point of view, as if you were meeting people for the very first time, or sitting up in that tree and seeing people differently. Ask that "nerd" to share some bubble fun (page 16) with you; invite the "mean" neighbor for tea (page 69); get to know one person from another race — just you and him or her. Aren't points of view amazing?

... AND THE LIVING IS EASY

No doubt about it: In summertime, the living really *is* easy.* There is a slightly slowed-down pace to summer. People take the time to put some flowers in an old vase, throw the ball to the dog, give Gram and Gramps an extra-big hug, and decide spontaneously to call the neighbors over for a family potluck barbecue. That's what we love about summer — there's so much to do and a feeling that, at least for a while, there's time to do it all!

* "Summertime, and the livin' is easy" is the opening line of the song "Summertime" from George Gershwin's opera *Porgy and Bess.*

WHISTLE A TUNE!

What's that tune just whistlin' around in your noggin? Let it out, kiddo! Let it hop, skip, and jump its way right out into the summer air. What's that, you say? It's trapped inside, and when you whistle nothing comes out but plain old tuneless air? Hang on, then, and we will have you whistlin' that happy tune before you can name all seven dwarfs (who, as you know, whistled their happy tune on their way to work each day).

P.S. If you already know how to whistle, go ahead and whistle right past this part. Next stop, "I always wanted to . . ." pages 108-109.

For a whistling good time, read *Whistle for Willie* by Ezra Jack Keats. Or, wet your whistle with the adventure tales on page 114.

summer reads

... AND THE LIVING IS EASY

WHISTLING
In Three Easy Steps

If you haven't learned to whistle yet, here's your chance! You've already got all you need — a great pair of lips and a healthy set of lungs. So, pucker up!

1. Shape your lips into a small "O," as if you're saying "Whoooo."

2. Place your tongue against each side of your upper back teeth.

3. Take a deep breath and then let it out, tightening your lips as the air escapes.

No Luck?

If the only sound that comes out is air, just keep trying! Try wetting your lips with your tongue. If you keep practicing, you'll soon hear a hint of a whistle. Before you know it, you'll be whistlin' all over town!

Whistle In . . .

Once you get the basic whistle down, you can learn to whistle as you breathe *in* as well as while you breathe *out*. That way, you'll be able to whistle whole songs without stopping to take air in. Aren't you just amazing?

I ALWAYS WANTED TO . . .

There are so many things to do, and summertime is such a great time to start doing them. Maybe it's whistling, maybe it's going fishing, maybe it's something that everyone else seemed to learn, but somehow it got by you. Maybe you want to feel better about yourself by doing something for others and by taking better care of yourself. Now's the time. Whatever the reason, speak up, my friend, because guess what? There are lots of people just wishing they could join you in your efforts, right now!

If you want to:	Ask at the:
Learn to swim	YMCA, YWCA, or the Red Cross
Play baseball or softball	Little League organization or your town's recreation department
Play the guitar or make music	music store, school, community band
Learn to read	library or a bookstore
Volunteer	the United Way, or your local hospital
Learn CPR and first aid	Red Cross
Learn to baby-sit	"Y," Red Cross, Scouts
Help the environment	local Audubon center, Sierra Club chapter, or town parks and recreation organization
Learn an "old-time" craft	senior citizens' housing or Grange
Walk people's dogs	put a sign up at a store, ask at a pet store
Make a difference	look through this book
Play soccer or lacrosse	recreation department or "Y"
Get in shape	"Y," health club, recreation department
Go on hikes	recreation department, sporting goods store
Go biking with others	recreation department, bike store
Make some friends	join a club, volunteer, visit the library
Make pottery	local arts and crafts store
Eat healthier	library for books on healthy eating, your doctor
Act in a play	school, local theater, community center, library

YAY!

To find places and people, look in the Yellow Pages under your subject, put up signs and look at signs at the library or your neighborhood store, call the parks department, the town hall, your school, or the high school.

If you can't pay for lessons, offer to *barter* (trade). If someone will teach you about making pottery, offer to clean the craft room after classes or baby-sit while other classes are being taught. If someone will teach you to read, maybe you can teach them something you know how to do – shoot baskets, for instance. When it is learning that you are after – whatever the subject, or sport, or craft – there is always someone who would be delighted to help you. Don't give up if you hit a "dead-end." Keep looking until you connect with just the right person. Great!

Root for the home team!

Have you ever been to a ball game? There are fans yelling in the stands, people eating hot dogs and drinking sodas, everyone talking and wearing baseball caps. Believe it or not, rooting for a home team (or any team) is great fun. All of these strangers get together in the stands and suddenly they have one thing in common — they want *their* team to win the game! You'll be on your feet cheering before you know it!

make a difference

Offer to wash someone's car.

Grab a bucket of warm water, some mild dishwashing detergent, a big sponge — and get washing away. Do a thorough job, because when it comes to car washing, a messy job is as bad as no washing at all. Once all the dirt has been sponged away, hose off the suds thoroughly (and yes, yourself and a friend, too), and then with clean rags, shine up the chrome! All that and no one even asked you? You really are the greatest! Thanks.

CLOUD MOODS

Be a giraffe, and spend the day with your head in the clouds!

summer reads

Get ready to visit "cloud nine" while reading some cloud-inspired stories like *Dreams* by Peter Spier, *Hi, Clouds* by Carol Greene, and *It Looked Like Spilt Milk* by Charles G. Shaw. Need a laugh? Read *Cloudy With a Chance of Meatballs* by Judi Barrett.

Name That Cloud!

Some clouds are light and wispy, others heavy and dark. Here is a very simple way to make sense out of what might seem, at first, to be nonsense.

Cloud-speak: Learn these five simple Latin words, and cloud names will make perfect sense!

Cirrus means a "curl or lock of hair."

Cumulus means "heap."

Stratus means "spread out."

Alto means "high."

Nimbus means "dark rain cloud."

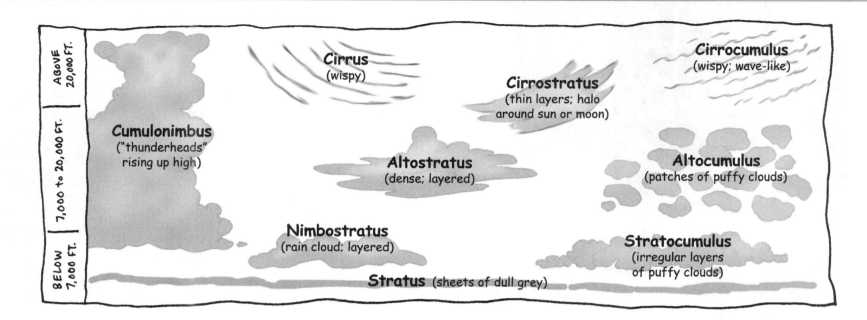

Above 20,000 ft.
7,000 to 20,000 ft.
Below 7,000 ft.

Cirrus (wispy)

Cirrostratus (thin layers; halo around sun or moon)

Cirrocumulus (wispy; wave-like)

Cumulonimbus ("thunderheads" rising up high)

Altostratus (dense; layered)

Altocumulus (patches of puffy clouds)

Nimbostratus (rain cloud; layered)

Stratocumulus (irregular layers of puffy clouds)

Stratus (sheets of dull grey)

SMART CLOUDS!

Should you and your friends sleep out tonight? Let the clouds tell you. Good day for a trip to the beach? Ask the clouds. These clouds aren't just hanging around for decoration; they can tell us what weather is on the way, and maybe even save the day!

☁ Wispy **cirrus clouds** high in the sky are the first sign of an approaching warm front. A warm front brings moisture, so rain may be on the way.

☁ **Stratus clouds** also often bring rain, and **nimbostratus clouds** are so thick and dark they completely block the sun.

☁ Puffy **cumulus clouds** (page 111) usually indicate fair weather, especially when there is plenty of space between them. So don't worry about rain when you're lying on the grass watching these clouds go by!

CLOUD-PAINTING

Have you ever gazed at the clouds and thought you were staring at a sky full of ice-cream cones, sheep, floating pillows, or sailboats? Well, cloud-painting is a fun way to extend your imagination after a day of cloud-gazing. "I spy with my little eye . . . feathers sailing on puffs of cotton candy!"

Now, it's your turn.

MATERIALS

- Food coloring
- Water
- Small containers or paper cups
- Paintbrushes (several sizes)
- Paper (textured watercolor paper is best)
- Fine-tip markers or pencil

LET'S DO IT!

For each watercolor, mix 3 drops of food coloring with 1 teaspoon (5 ml) water. To paint clouds, paint random blobs and strokes of watercolor on a sheet of wet paper. Change colors as often as you like.

When your paint clouds are dry, *suggest* details sparingly with a small brush, or markers, or pencil. For example, if a splotch looks like a bird, you might add shape to the beak with a darker color, or soft little brush strokes to "fill in" the feathery wings. You want to paint the *impression* of what you see, just as it is in the sky.

GREAT SUMMERTIME READS

Get yourself some good books as you head for your hammock, a patch of grass—or anywhere! Summertime is a great time to read—just for the fun of it! Join the summer reading program at your local library. Or, just choose some books about your favorite subject. Do you like suspense and mysteries, or books about kids in silly situations? Do you like books that show you how to build things or how to set up your aquarium? Whatever your interests, you can read all about them! Fresh out of ideas? Here are a few of our favorites for your reading pleasure:

Harry Potter and the Sorcerer's Stone by J.K. Rowling

The BFG and *Matilda* by Roald Dahl

In the Year of the Boar and Jackie Robinson by Bette Bao Lord

The Giver by Lois Lowry

The Last of the Really Great Whangdoodles by Julie Edwards

Gone-Away Lake by Elizabeth Enright

The Enchanted Castle by E. Nesbit

Magic or Not? by Edward Eager

Jip: His Story by Katherine Peterson

Officer Buckle and Gloria by Peggy Rathmann

The View From Saturday by E.L. Konigsburg

The Midwife's Apprentice by Karen Cushman

Golem by David Wisniewski

Which book is your favorite? Ask your librarian or favorite bookstore to start a listing of local kids' favorite books. You'll get lots of good ideas of what to read from people with similar interests to yours.

SUMMER 'N' SAND

Sand and summer go together whether you build castles on the beach or sand villages in a sandbox.

And, sand-painting is an age-old tradition from the Native American Navajo people of Northern New Mexico and Arizona. Here, you'll glue down your art, whereas the Navajo let the wind pick up the glistening grains of sand and blow them away.

PAINT WITH SAND (or rice)

Create lots of different colors, and choose any images you feel like working with — wildlife, beachscapes, landscapes, flashy cars, city scenes, your name, or geometric shapes are all great themes. It's creativity at its best, because it is created by *you!*

MATERIALS

- Heavy drawing paper, pencil
- Cookie sheet or tray
- White glue, water, spoon
- Paper cup or other small container
- Paintbrush
- Sand (or rice), two or more colors (see page 116)

LET'S DO IT!

1. Lightly draw your design on the paper. Set the paper on the cookie sheet or tray.
2. Mix a spoonful of glue and a spoonful of water together in the cup.
3. Thinking of the lightest color, paint glue on all areas where you want that one color of sand to stick.
4. Use a spoon or your fingers to sprinkle that color sand over the glue. Make sure every bit of glue is covered. Let sand set for a few moments.
5. Gently turn the paper over the tray and tap to let the extra sand fall off. Pour the extra sand back into its container to use again.
6. Let the color set for about 10 minutes; then, repeat steps 3, 4, and 5 with the next darkest color. Continue until you've used all your colors.

115

SAND-PAINTING PARTICULARS

Making your own colored sand or rice is very easy. No need to buy any fancy kits, either!

MATERIALS

For each color:

- ¼ cup (50 ml) water or rubbing alcohol
- Food coloring
- Container with lid for each color
- ½ cup (125 ml) clean, sifted sand or rice
- Bucket and sieve
- Newspaper

LET'S DO IT!

1. Mix water and several drops of food coloring in the container. Add more coloring for a deeper color. Or, ask a grown-up to help you use alcohol (it dries faster than water). Add the sand or rice. Stir the mixture until evenly coated.

2. Let the sand or rice sit in the colored water for at least 15 minutes (about 5 minutes for rice). Then, using the sieve, carefully pour the extra water into the bucket. Spread out sand or rice on newspaper to dry.

Large impressions: Sand-painting works best if you create an impression with color, rather than trying to capture small details. For red flowers in a field, you might paint red blobs, instead of showing petals, stems, and leaves.

Desert look: Sand-paint on sandpaper to make your artwork look as if it's sitting on desert sand.

Smooth or jagged geometrics: When you sketch shapes, decide if you want jagged geometric shapes colliding into one another, or smooth, circular shapes oozing into one another. Use color to dramatize the differences.

Refrigerator magnet: Cut cardboard or cardboard-backed sandpaper into small shapes and sand-paint them. Seal with clear acrylic sealer. Glue a magnet on the back.

SANDSCAPE IN A JAR

Make an artscape in a jar to keep on your desk or bookcase by carefully layering colored sand or rice in a small jar.

The basics: Spoon or funnel a layer of colored sand into a nicely shaped small jar. Gently tap the jar to level the sand. Continue adding layers of different-colored sands until you reach the top, tapping after each new layer. Screw on the lid. If you've filled the jar to the very top, the sand won't be disturbed when you move it.

Rainbow jar: Layer colors in the order of the rainbow: red, orange, yellow, green, blue, indigo, violet (remember ROY G. BIV?).

Varied layers: Vary the widths of the layers, or tilt the jar to slant the layers.

Patterns: Gently slide a knitting needle down the side of the jar through the layers of sand; then, slowly pull it out. (Be careful not to overmix.) The sand layers gradually overlap and blend, making an interesting pattern of colorful waves and ripples.

Cool...

117

BACKYARD TROPICAL BEACH PARTY!

Put on the calypso music, grab a flowered shirt hidden at the back of Dad's or Mom's closet, mix up a Cool Watermelon Slush, and head for the Tropics—the backyard tropics, that is, for some summertime fun!

P.S. No backyard? We know you can come up with a safe and fun option. (Look in *Tar Beach* by Faith Ringgold for some more ideas!)

What to wear

Sunglasses
Bathing suits
Hawaiian shirts
Skirts made of raffia (Easy to make out of wide crepe paper or newspaper. Just open a few pages of newspaper and cut from bottom to top, leaving 1 inch/2.5 cm at top for waist-band.)

What to bring

Sunscreen
Beach towels
Sun hat (or make your own, see page 44)

What to eat and drink

Tropical fruit: slices of pineapple, mango, banana, coconut
Freshly squeezed orange juice. Serve in a tall plastic cup with ice cubes and bendy straws.
Cool Watermelon Slushes (see page 120)

What to do

Make Leis

Ask permission to gather small, sturdy flowers, such as strawflowers, dandelions, or daisies. Thread a needle with a 24-inch (60-cm) length of thread and double it. Thread the blossoms onto the thread, tie the ends, and wear. (No flowers to pick? Plan ahead and ask a florist if you may use some flowers that have gone by.)

Do the Limbo

Turn on the "Limbo Rock" single or any music with a calypso beat. Take turns sliding (legs and stomach first) under a broomstick held at one height. No ducking under! Anyone who touches the bar or the ground with his or her hands is out! Lower the bar after each round until you have a limbo winner.

Draw a Sidewalk Tropical Mural

Use sidewalk chalk to draw tropical fish, waves, palm trees, shells, and beachcombers on the sidewalk. Or, if you're really at the beach, build sand castles!

Play "Go Fish"

Grab a deck of cards. You know the rules!

Sunbathe

Slather on plenty of sunscreen, grab a hat, and catch some rays!

Make a Coconut Shell Bowl

Enjoy that fresh coconut and then make a very special bowl (see page 120).

COOL WATERMELON SLUSHES

Drinking watermelon? That's right! This thick, icy slush is oh so refreshing that you'll add it to your favorite ways to eat watermelon.

P.S. Don't forget to buy *seedless* watermelon!

Making slushes: Put about 6 ice cubes in a blender or food processor. Ask a grown-up to mix the ice cubes until they're crushed. Add about 2 cups (500 ml) of seedless watermelon pieces and blend until the shake is slushy, about 1 minute. Add about a tablespoon (15 ml) of sugar or honey and blend for 10 seconds. Pour the slush into tall glasses, and slurp to your heart's content!

Spit It Out!

The world record for watermelon seed spitting is 65 feet and 4 inches (20 meters)! How close can you and your friends come to this record? Try it (outdoors, of course) on some hot summer day, and then rinse off — and cool off — under the hose!

Ptooey!

Make a Coconut Shell Bowl

There is nothing quite as delicious as fresh coconut! And, a coconut shell, cut in half (you'll need a grown-up to help you), makes two perfectly round bowls — great containers for a cool tropical drink, a dish of ice cream, or for holding paper clips and other odds and ends.

Bake the coconut halves in a 300°F (150°C) oven for 10 minutes, or until you can remove the nutmeat easily from the shell. Use sandpaper to smooth the outside of the shell. Wash and dry, inside and outside.

CELEBRATE THE GREAT OUTDOORS!

There's a whole big, beautiful world outdoors. It's yours to enjoy, to hop and skip in, to care for, to share with others and all of nature's animal friends. It's a treasure as precious as life itself. If ever there were cause to celebrate, the great outdoors on a summer day just about shouts, "Hip, hip, hooray! Celebrate!"

YAY!

TREES, GLORIOUS TREES!

W hether you like to sit under them or in them, swing from them, climb in them, hide behind them, talk to them, play in their autumn leaves, listen to them rustle, or enjoy their shade, trees are cause for celebration.

The Seventh Generation

O ne of the very important ideas Native Americans hold is that we all "borrow the earth from our children." Whenever they had to make a decision about how to use the land they lived on, they would ask, "How will this affect the children of the coming seven generations?"

It's an amazing question, because in its simple message is a very serious truth: We all have a choice to leave the earth better than we found it, or to destroy it bit by bit. Encourage your family and friends to ask this question every day, and follow this Native American tradition as you celebrate the great outdoors this summer!

Visit an arboretum.

Visit a what, you say? An arboretum is a special kind of nature preserve where beautiful and unusual species of trees are grown. Depending on when you visit and where you live, you'll see hundreds of trees in bloom, smell their beautiful fragrances, and see a wonderful array of tree sizes, shapes, leaves, and bark. Bring some bark rubbing supplies (plain paper and crayons) and have a tree-mendous time!

... out & about

make a difference

Plant a tree for World Environment Day.

The United Nations Environment Program's efforts are honored by planting trees each year on June 5 (or whenever it is a good time for planting where you live). Plant a tree on your property, at your school, or in your community. A local garden nursery can help you choose good "growers" and offer planting instructions. Here's to healthy trees and cleaner air everywhere!

summer reads

How do people express their love for nature? Some write poems about their feelings! Read Barbara Brenner's poem "The Earth Is Painted Green," or "Hurt No Living Thing" by Christina Rossetti. Or, celebrate your trees with Kristine O'Connell's *Old Elm Speaks: Tree Poems*.

Like all living creatures, trees need air, water, and food. But if their roots are covered with concrete, or if the soil they're growing in lacks nutrients, or if they don't get enough rainwater, city trees will die. You and your friends can actually save trees' lives! Grab a litter bag and work gloves, and begin by clearing out any litter that's under the tree.

FIRST AID FOR CITY TREES

If your trees could talk, they might very well be shouting, "Feed me! Water me! Love me!" That's especially true of trees planted along sidewalks and curbs. But, *you* can be a tree rescuer and best friend, too. Yes, *you* can make all the difference!

All We Need Is Love and . . .

SLURP!
SLURP!

a healthy meal! Sprinkle some nutrition around with *natural materials* like fallen leaves, grass clippings, and rotted compost. These natural materials protect the tree in winter. By spring, it all breaks down into a yummy tree feast that's absorbed by the roots.

Trees need plenty of *water* — about 6 gallons (24 L) twice a week right through the fall, a time when trees often die of thirst. So it's glug, glug, glug. And, if you find some *earthworms* in the park, bring a few of them to your tree, because, besides you, earthworms are the soil's best friend.

Wow! Be proud of the care you've shown your tree. Enjoy a picnic beneath its boughs with a friend. Sit in its shade, rest against its sturdy trunk, and share the perfect tree-and-me story, Shel Silverstein's *The Giving Tree* or *The Great Kapok Tree* by Lynne Cherry.

MAKE A LITTER PICKER-UPPER

Don't like handling litter? Can't say we blame you. You can make a handy litter picker-upper. With grown-up help, drive a headless nail into the end of a stick, and presto! You're in the tree-rescuing business. Terrific!

Start a Kids' Clean-Up Club

Show your love for the environment by starting a Kids for a Clean Environment (Kids F.A.C.E.) club this summer. Kids F.A.C.E. was founded by Melissa Poe, a kid from Nashville, Tennessee, to help stop pollution in the United States. There are hundreds of Kids F.A.C.E. chapters across the country, and there's one waiting to be started by *you* and *your friends*. For information, write Melissa Poe at Kids F.A.C.E., P.O. Box 158254, Nashville, TN 37215, or check out http://members.aol.com/pforpeace/KidsFACE/.

Two Points!

MARVELOUS MUD

Ooey, gooey, soft and cool. Mud is marvelous — one of Mother Nature's summer treasures that kids love to celebrate by plunging their squishing fingers and wriggling toes deep into the stuff. P.S. If any grown-up scolds, just explain that you are using nature's original paint to make beautiful art!

MAKE A MUDCLOTH

Make a mudcloth to hang from a clothesline or some wire in your room, or to make into a banner with a dowel. These cloths make beautiful paintings in a very primitive style.

To clean mud: Place a strainer over an empty coffee can. Scoop in some mud or dry dirt. Run water through the strainer, letting mud and water sink to the bottom of the can. Throw out debris from the strainer, pour off some of the water, and repeat the process until mud is clean.

To make the mud paint: Add about ¹/₂ cup (125 ml) brown and ¹/₂ cup (125 ml) blue tempera paint to about a cup (250 ml) of cleaned mud in a coffee can. Stir well. This is enough paint to make several mudcloths.

To paint cloth: Draw a very bold and simple design and a border in pencil on a piece of white cotton cloth, like an old sheet, about 9 inches by 12 inches (22.5 cm by 30 cm). Double-line the pencil drawing and fill in with mud to make the painting easier. Using a variety of tools, such as a spoon's back, small branches and twigs, and sharp and flat rocks, apply the mud paint to your design. Hang to display.

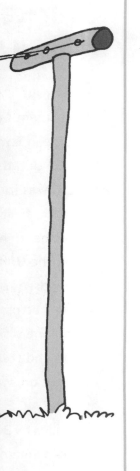

BEACH FUN

make a difference

Keep it clean!
Sad to say, but you may find plain old litter along with nature's treasures at the beaches near oceans, lakes, and rivers. Believe it or not, some people actually leave their garbage on the beach. You know better, so lend a helping hand. Whenever you're at the beach, bring along a bag to pick up some litter — yours and someone else's. Thank you.

Going to the beach is just about the coolest thing you can do in the summer. Bring along a bucket, a sieve, and a net for beachtime fun, and look in the sand and mud for critter clues. Then, celebrate the sand, sun, and flowing water! Except for the ocean tide activity, you can do these activities at a lake, pond, river, or park.

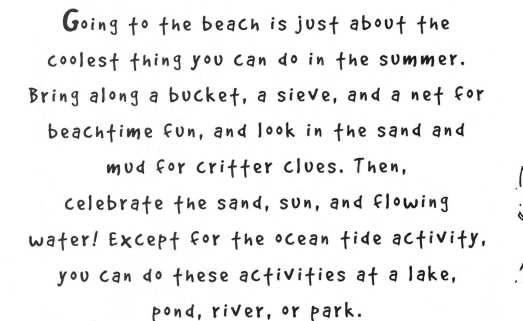

HERE COMES THE TIDE!

High tide is when the level of the ocean rises; low tide is when it falls. The tides are caused by the pull of the moon's gravity, tugging at the water here on Earth. The ocean changes from high tide to low tide twice a day.

For the best beachcombing: Check tide pools right after the tide goes out, during low tide. That's when you'll find all the treasures the high tide left behind. (Plan your beach trip for low tide. Check the seaside local paper for tides.)

Tide pool rule: When the ocean begins to surge back in, it's time to go. Don't linger. The tide pool you are visiting will soon be at the bottom of the ocean!

Strand lines: Look along flat, sandy beaches for the strand lines that mark the high tides. After a storm, this is a good place to hunt for nature's sea treasures.

Thanks to the fish hatcheries, which stock thousands of our nation's rivers and lakes with fish, there's plenty of good fishing for everyone. Most hatcheries offer tours of their facilities, so call your state's Department of Fish and Wildlife for information on visiting a hatchery in your area. If you're lucky, you'll get to visit during feeding time and watch the water "boil" with finned swimmers!

... out & about

PLAY CRAB RELAY!

Be a crab! Be a crab! (Notice we *didn't* say, "Be crabby!") Here's a fun game to play at the beach — or in your own backyard!

Divide into teams. The first one in each line — the crab — sits on the floor, back towards the finish line. At the "go" signal, the crab walks backwards on hands and feet, lifting hips off the ground. When the crab reaches the finish line, he or she stands up, runs back, and tags the next crab, who then takes a turn. The first team of crabs to finish wins. But don't be crabby if you lose — it's just for fun!

SPLAT!

FINISH

CELEBRATE SUMMER!

Gather a group of friends and neighbors for an old-time, fun-time summer potluck celebration, complete with games, a scavenger hunt, and your favorite summer foods. Invite friends, family, and folks on your city block or in your neighborhood to join in the fun.

SHARE THE FEAST

Ask each person to prepare a favorite summer food to share at your summer gathering. They should bring enough for twice as many people (family of four brings enough for eight). This way, there will be plenty of food and beverages.

Roasted Corn-in-its-Husk: Perhaps this can be your surprise. Ask a grown-up to help you prepare the outdoor grill. Soak ears of corn, husk and all, in water for at least 15 minutes. Set them on the grill and cover. Rotate corn while it cooks (about 12 minutes). Once cooked, peel the husk and silk carefully — the corn will be very hot and steamy — but absolutely delicious! Summer never tasted so good!

Summer fun Tablecloth Mural

Cover a picnic table with two long sheets of butcher paper, shiny side down. Tape down the paper with masking tape, so it doesn't blow away. Set out markers and crayons. Now, gather everyone around to draw his or her favorite things about summertime. Then, put out the food, and let the celebration of good times with good friends begin!

GAMES GALORE!

What's a celebration without some good, old, fun-time games and contests? Here's how to have lots of thrills, spills, and bushels of laughs!

Hula Hoop Toss: Can you ring a hula hoop around a watermelon? Mark scores on three to five watermelons, with the highest score farthest from the starting line. Players stand at the line and toss the hula hoop around the melons with three tries each.

Melon Slalom: Place watermelons in two rows (about 15 yards/15 m) from a starting line. Form two teams. The first player of each team weaves through the row of melons, returns to the starting line, and tags the next teammate. The first team to complete the slalom wins. Then, it's time to have a watermelon seed-spitting contest (see page 120).

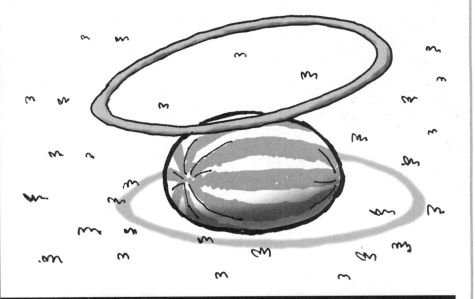

Three-Legged Race: Form two teams, grouping players by threes. Tie each group of three together by their legs, using bandannas. Place a watermelon at the end of the course. At the word "Go," have one group from each team run to the melon and back. The first team to have all its players complete the course wins.

No-Hands Pie-Eating Contest: If you've never tried this, get ready for some good summer fun! Bake or buy one mini-pie per contestant. Set the pies outside on a table. The players should sit on their hands. Someone says "Go," and the players dig in — face first! — in a race to eat their pies. The first clean plate wins!

As night draws near, gather your friends in a circle,
tell tales, recount great (and imagined) experiences,
talk about what makes summer so special, and sing some songs.
Because summer is definitely something to sing about!

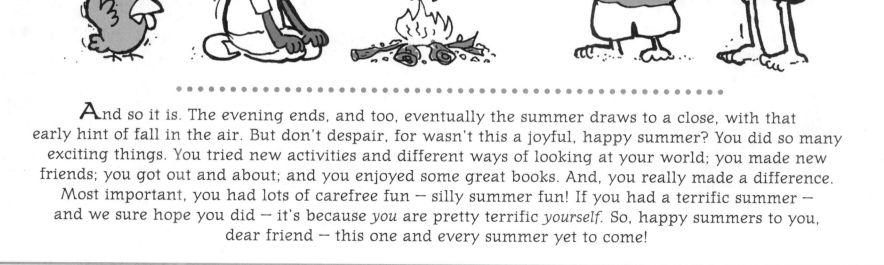

And so it is. The evening ends, and too, eventually the summer draws to a close, with that early hint of fall in the air. But don't despair, for wasn't this a joyful, happy summer? You did so many exciting things. You tried new activities and different ways of looking at your world; you made new friends; you got out and about; and you enjoyed some great books. And, you really made a difference. Most important, you had lots of carefree fun — silly summer fun! If you had a terrific summer — and we sure hope you did — it's because *you* are pretty terrific *yourself*. So, happy summers to you, dear friend — this one and every summer yet to come!

INDEX

A

activities. *See* art activities; building projects; crafts; indoor activities; Make a Difference projects; nature activities; Out & About; outdoor activities; water activities
American Sign Language (ASL), 56–59
ants, 49
art activities
  bubble prints, 17
  cloud-paintings, 113
  face/body painting, 4, 12–14
  jam jar labels, 48
  lampshade, moon-&-stars, 76
  moon phases flip book, 78
  mudcloth, 126
  photo statue, 92
  pitter-patter (rain) paintings, 55
  sand/rice painting, 115–116
  sandscape in a jar, 117
  self-portrait, 91–92
  sidewalk tropical mural, 119
  spider's web, preserving a, 30
  sun banner, 45
  sunrise paintings, with sparkle paints, 44
  sunrise silhouettes, 43
  tablecloth mural, 130
  wax-resist nightscape painting, 79
  See also crafts

B

bats, 31–34
beach, 127–129. *See also* outdoor activities, tropical beach party
beverages. *See* drink recipes
books
  handmade, 104
  reading suggestions. *See* Summer Reads
  See also libraries
boomerangs, 8
bubbles, 15–17
bugs, 22–32, 49
building projects
  cap rack, 97
  desk organizer, 96
  litter picker-upper, 125
  puppet theaters, 66, 68
  rain gauge, 53
  stilts, 3
  toad playground, 36
  water slide, 18
  See also crafts

C

camping, 82–89
caricatures, 92
circus, 4–5
clouds, 111–113
communication, 55–62
conservation, 122–124
cookies, 9–10, 71, 77
cooking. *See* recipes: foods & drinks; recipes: non-edible
crafts
  books, handmade, 104
  boomerangs, 8
  bubble wands and blowers, 15–16
  can-walkers, 2
  coconut shell bowl, 120
  desk organizer, 96
  finger-knitting, cat's-tail, 99
  hopping (paper) toads, 38
  keychain, knotted, 100
  leis, 119
  puppets, 64–65, 67
  refrigerator magnet, sand painting, 116
  shadow puppets, 67
  sleeping bag, make your own, 83
  solar system scale model, 80
  sun hats, paper, 44
  T-shirts, decorated, 72
  T-shirts, tie-dyed, 73–74
  yo-yo, 7
  See also art activities; building projects
crickets, 28

D

dancing, 100–102
deaf/hearing-impaired people, communicating with, 56–59
drink recipes, 9, 21, 69, 71, 120

E

echolocation, 34
events to attend. *See* Out & About

F

face/body painting, 4, 12–14
food. *See* recipes: foods & drinks
friendship, 71

G

games
  Crab Relay, 129
  Grandma Is Strange, 88
  Hula Hoop Toss, 131
  invent your own, 6
  Limbo, 119
  Melon Slalom, 131
  Moon-Star, 88
  "mosquito" guessing jar, 31
  No-Hands Pie-Eating Contest, 131
  Radar Game, 34
  Riddle Fortune Cookies, 9–10
  "sun" word charades, 51
  Three-Legged Race, 131
  Twenty Questions, 86
  Water Balloon Toss, 19
  Water Brigade, 19
  See also toys
ghost stories, 86
Gooblek, 19

H

hand shadows, 68, 87
hot-weather suggestions, 20. *See also* water activities

I

"I always wanted to . . . ," 107–108
ice cream, 21, 62–63
indoor activities
  American Sign Language (ASL), 56–59
  ballet class, 102
  bat-fomercial, create a, 33

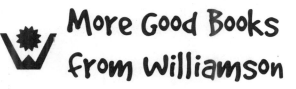

More Good Books from Williamson

See last page for ordering information, or visit your favorite bookseller. Thank you.

Williamson *Kids Can!*® Books

The following award-winning *Kids Can!*® books are for children ages 6 to 12. Each book is 144–176 pages, fully illustrated, trade paper, 11 x 8½, $12.95 US.

Parent's Guide Children's Media Award
Parents' Choice Approved

BOREDOM BUSTERS!
The Curious Kids' Activity Book
by Avery Hart & Paul Mantell

Parents' Choice Gold Award
Dr. Toy Best Vacation Product

THE KIDS' NATURE BOOK
365 Indoor/Outdoor Activities and Experiences
by Susan Milord

Parents' Choice Approved
Dr. Toy Best Vacation Product

KIDS GARDEN!
The Anytime, Anyplace Guide to Sowing & Growing Fun
by Avery Hart and Paul Mantell

Parents' Choice Recommended
American Bookseller Pick of the Lists

ADVENTURES IN ART
Art & Craft Experiences for 8- to 13-Year-Olds
by Susan Milord

Dr. Toy Best Vacation Product
American Bookseller Pick of the Lists

KIDS' CRAZY ART CONCOCTIONS
50 Mysterious Mixtures for Art & Craft Fun
by Jill Frankel Hauser

Parent's Guide Children's Media Award
Parents' Choice Approved

MAKING COOL CRAFTS & AWESOME ART!
A Kids' Treasure Trove of Fabulous Fun
by Roberta Gould

Selection of Book-of-the-Month;
Scholastic Book Clubs

KIDS COOK!
Fabulous Food for the Whole Family
by Sarah Williamson and Zachary Williamson

Parents' Choice Gold Award
American Bookseller Pick of the Lists
Oppenheim Toy Portfolio Best Book Award

THE KIDS' MULTICULTURAL ART BOOK
Art & Craft Experiences from Around the World
by Alexandra M. Terzian

Benjamin Franklin Best Multicultural Book Award
Skipping Stones Multicultural Honor Award

THE KIDS' MULTICULTURAL COOKBOOK
Food & Fun Around the World
by Deanna F. Cook

Children's Book-of-the-Month Club Selection

KIDS' COMPUTER CREATIONS
Using Your Computer for Art & Craft Fun
by Carol Sabbeth

Parent's Guide Children's Media Award
Benjamin Franklin Best Education/Teaching Book Award

HAND-PRINT ANIMAL ART
by Carolyn Carreiro
full color, $14.95

Parents' Choice Gold Award
Benjamin Franklin Best Juvenile Nonfiction Award

KIDS MAKE MUSIC!
Clapping and Tapping from Bach to Rock
by Avery Hart and Paul Mantell

American Bookseller Pick of the Lists
Oppenheim Toy Portfolio Best Book Award

EcoArt!
Earth-Friendly Art & Craft Experiences for 3- to 9-Year-Olds
by Laurie Carlson

THE KIDS' WILDLIFE BOOK
Exploring Animal Worlds through Indoor/Outdoor Crafts & Experiences
by Warner Shedd

SUMMER FUN!

HANDS AROUND THE WORLD
365 Creative Ways to Build Cultural Awareness & Global Respect
by Susan Milord

Parents' Choice Approved
KIDS CREATE!
Art & Craft Experiences for 3- to 9-Year-Olds
by Laurie Carlson

American Bookseller Pick of the Lists
Oppenheim Toy Portfolio Best Book Award
Benjamin Franklin Best Juvenile Nonfiction
Teachers' Choice Award
SUPER SCIENCE CONCOCTIONS
50 Mysterious Mixtures for Fabulous Fun
by Jill Frankel Hauser

Oppenheim Toy Portfolio Best Book Award
American Bookseller Pick of the Lists
THE KIDS' SCIENCE BOOK
Creative Experiences for Hands-On Fun
by Robert Hirschfeld and Nancy White

Parent's Guide Children's Media Award
Teachers' Choice Award
CUT-PAPER PLAY!
Dazzling Creations from Construction Paper
by Sandi Henry

Early Childhood News Directors' Choice Award
VROOM! VROOM!
Making 'dozers, 'copters, trucks & more
by Judy Press

Parents Magazine Parents' Pick
KIDS LEARN AMERICA!
Bringing Geography to Life with People, Places, & History
by Patricia Gordon and Reed C. Snow

THE KIDS' NATURAL HISTORY BOOK
Making Dinos, Fossils, Mummies & Zulu Huts
by Judy Press

GIZMOS & GADGETS
Creating Science Contraptions that Work (& Knowing Why)
by Jill Frankel Hauser

Williamson's Kaleidoscope Kids™ Books

Kaleidoscope Kids™ books encourage kids, ages 7-12, to explore places, subjects, peoples, and history from many different perspectives, using many different skills. Each book is 96-104 pages, two-color, fully illustrated, 10 x 10, $10.95.

Children's Book Council Notable Book
American Bookseller Pick of the Lists
Dr. Toy 10 Best Educational Products
PYRAMIDS!
50 Hands-On Activities to Experience Ancient Egypt
by Avery Hart & Paul Mantell

Parent's Guide Children's Media Award
American Bookseller Pick of the Lists
KNIGHTS & CASTLES
50 Hands-On Activities to Experience the Middle Ages
by Avery Hart & Paul Mantell

ANCIENT GREECE!
40 Hands-On Activities to Experience This Wondrous Age
by Avery Hart and Paul Mantell

MEXICO!
40 Activities to Experience Mexico Past and Present
by Susan Milord

BRIDGES!
Amazing Structures to Design, Build & Test
by Elizabeth Rieth and Carol Johmann

GEOLOGY ROCKS!
50 Hands-On Activities to Explore the Earth
by Cindy Blobaum

THE BEAST IN YOU!
Activities & Questions to Explore Evolution
by Marc McCutcheon

and there's more...!

Williamson's *Tales Alive!*® Books . . .

A feast of folklore fun for ages 4 and up! These beautiful, full-color books focus on retellings of multicultural folktales accompanied by original paintings and activities to round out a child's understanding of a tale and its subject. Books are 96-128 pages, full color with original art, 8½ x 11.

Benjamin Franklin Best Juvenile Fiction
Parents' Choice Honor Award
Skipping Stones Multicultural Honor Award

TALES ALIVE!
Ten Multicultural Folktales with Activities
by Susan Milord
Trade paper, $15.95

Benjamin Franklin Best Juvenile Fiction
Benjamin Franklin Best Multicultural Book Award
Teachers' Choice Award

TALES OF THE SHIMMERING SKY
Ten Global Folktales with Activities
by Susan Milord
Trade paper, $15.95

TALES ALIVE!
BIRD TALES
from Near and Far
by Susan Milord
Trade paper, $14.95

Visit our Website:
http://www.williamsonbooks.com
or, call 800-234-8791 for catalog.

To order Books

Williamson books are available from your favorite bookseller, or directly from Williamson Publishing.

Toll-free phone orders: **800-234-8791**
Visa or Mastercard accepted.
E-mail orders with charge card: **orders@williamsonbooks.com**
Or, send check or money order to:

WILLIAMSON PUBLISHING

P.O. Box 185, Charlotte, Vermont 05445

Postage is $3.20 for first book plus $.50 for each additional book. Satisfaction is guaranteed or full refund without questions or quibbles. Books shipped within 48 hours.

Prices may be slightly higher when purchased in Canada.

Kids Can!®, *Little Hands*®, and *Tales Alive!*® are registered trademarks of Williamson Publishing. *Kaleidoscope Kids*™ and *Good Times!*™ are trademarks of Williamson Publishing.